LE CREUSET®

The Cast Iron way to Cook

Sue Cutts

SIMON & SCHUSTER
A VIACOM COMPANY

My sincere thanks go to Faye Gooding, Senior Vice President of Retail and Legal Affairs, Le Creuset of America, for giving me the opportunity to write this book and to Audrey Gaudrault for her enormous help. I am also indebted to my family, David and Graham for their patience and perseverance in tasting and vetting the recipes, and producing the manuscript. Thanks also to Jan Odam of Cyprus, Texas, for her advice and re-testing of recipes in America.

First published by Simon & Schuster UK Ltd, 2001
A Viacom Company

With thanks to Wendy Veale for the following recipes:
Traditional Cheese Fondue (Fondue Neuchâtel), Creamy Mushroom Fondue, Indian-Style Fondue with Crudités, Crab Fondue, Bitter Chocolate & Orange Fondue, Fondue Bourguignonne, and Jamaican Calypso Fondue.

1 3 5 7 9 10 8 6 4 2

Simon & Schuster UK Ltd
Africa House
64–78 Kingsway
London WC2B 6AH

A CIP catalogue record for this book is available from the British Library.

ISBN 0 85941 995 9

Design by Ocean Blue Design, Surrey
Photography by Steve Baxter
Typeset by Textype, Cambridge
Printed and bound in Hong Kong

Symbols Guide

 This symbol denotes a Le Creuset Tip and it will inform you about any other Le Creuset pans which may be suitable for a particular recipe.

 This symbol denotes a Cook's Tip and contains extra information about preparing and cooking the recipes.

 This symbol denotes a Wine Tip and tells you what type of wines are most suitable for enjoying with a particular recipe.

CONTENTS

HERITAGE

For over 75 years, Le Creuset Cast Iron Cookware has been manufactured at a foundry in the town of Fresnoy le Grand approximately 120 miles north-east of Paris. Set among rolling hills and arable landscapes, the world's largest, and oldest, manufacturer of high quality cast iron cookware distributes Le Creuset to every corner of the globe.

This region of France has been associated with the casting of cookware for over four centuries and Cousances was the first established foundry in the town known by that name in 1553. It is documented that "for 7 hogshead of wheat", Jehan Barisien obtained from the Lord of the Manor of Cousances the right to cast iron in a location called "God's Fountain". Subsequently he was granted the Cousances Coat of Arms and therefore the right to use the name.

One of the first cooking utensils ever produced was called a Cocotte. It is a cast iron French oven and this shape, and indeed the name, was the pivot of what is now an extensive range of cookware.

When the Le Creuset foundry was opened in 1925 it was able to learn from, and utilize much of the experience and crafting skills developed over centuries of Cousances production. Cousances had not only made cookware but many other pieces too, such as stoves, fireplace surrounds and ornate pillars for street lighting.

However, Le Creuset was to be the first foundry completely dedicated to the production of cookware and it has maintained that status ever since. From 1956 to 1992, the two foundries worked in tandem until, in 1992, Cousances production was transferred to Fresnoy le Grand where the size of the site was able to cater for the technical developments demanded today.

Not least of these new developments is the change to environmental standards for production which, hundreds of years ago, were not even contemplated. Coal and coke are no longer used for the furnaces; electricity has taken their place. Modern fuel and technology have eliminated smoke from the atmosphere and new cleansing techniques have resulted in cleaner by-products leaving the foundry.

However, some things have not changed and probably the most important thing is the continued commitment to hand-crafted techniques for the process following the molding of the shape. Each piece begins life in its own sand mold, destroyed after each use, and this means, of course, that each piece is "individual" and can be very slightly different to its neighbour in the next mold. Once released from the mold, and until it reaches its packaging, fifteen different pairs of hands and eyes scrutinize each piece, checking for flaws and imperfections, perfecting the edges, curves and handles. This level of craftsmanship is only learnt with years of experience and is vital for maintaining the high standards for which Le Creuset is so well known.

As one would expect, there are some areas where computer-aided technology has revolutionized production. For example, both the cast iron and the porcelain enamel are scientifically monitored to a greater degree than ever before. Both have their own secret and special "recipe" which is closely guarded by just a few personnel and checked constantly.

All the porcelain enamels such as basecoat, color and satin black on each piece of Le Creuset are made from small glass silica chips which are ground to a powder and mixed with other ingredients, water and, of course, a "color". This mixture, when fired (vitrified) at over 1,600°F, produces the very hard, glossy enamel for which Le Creuset has an unrivalled reputation. The porcelain enamel is generally put on in two layers. The first is a clear coat which completely seals the raw cast iron, lid rims and pan rims included, while the second layer gives color, strength and durability to the whole piece including the base. The market for glass-topped stoves requires cookware that is as smooth on the base as is possible and the strength and smoothness of Le Creuset's porcelain enamel makes it an ideal finish.

Some porcelain enamels are satin black and have a slightly more "grainy" texture. They are intentionally different and are better suited to the higher temperatures the surface reaches when searing, broiling and wok cooking. You will, therefore, find satin black on the inside of skillet grills, skillets and woks. All the porcelain enamels which are used conform to the Food and Drug Administration standards for food safety.

No range of cookware would be complete without some nonstick shapes and the use of one of the world's best known and most reliable coatings make the release of any food simplicity itself.

One of the huge advantages of entirely porcelain enamelled cast iron cookware is that when you take it home it is, after an initial wash, ready for use. There is no need to season any surface or keep it oiled between uses; it is simply used as the recipe dictates.

A unique and endearing quality of cast iron cookware is that it can be "molded" into almost any shape you desire. In terms of cookware this has, over the years, given Le Creuset the opportunity to produce a wide range of shapes. Some of the shapes are traditional and practical, such as the wok; some have an element of fun, such as the heart-shaped dish or pumpkin but all have the same outstanding qualities and heritage that simply sets Le Creuset apart.

Bonne Cuisine!

INTRODUCTION

For centuries, the kitchen has been the true "comfort zone" in the majority of homes, whatever the size or shape of the home. There can be few of us who don't appreciate the aromas of a gently simmering casserole or a freshly baked cake, especially when returning from a hard day's work or play. Producing good, wholesome and nutritious meals does not have to mean hours in the kitchen, indeed most of us these days don't have a lot of time to cook during the week and can only spend time cooking, experimenting and trying new recipes at weekends. This book intends, with the help of Le Creuset Cast Iron Cookware, to open up to you the vast repertoire of recipes this durable range of cookware can achieve, and in many cases achieve in minutes rather than in hours.

Historically, cast iron has been the prime material chosen for cooking vessels. Evidence of this can be seen in heritage centers all over the world. The Romans, for example, used cast iron for their cooking pots and only recently I saw examples of these so well preserved that they were immediately recognizable.

Durability is, of course, the most obvious benefit of cast iron and many pieces are actually handed down from one generation to the next. There is something quite comforting about making the same recipe in the same pot your mother or grandmother used, especially if you are cooking for your own family.

But durability is not its only strength. It cooks very evenly, distributing heat throughout the piece so that every corner or curve achieves the same temperature. It is just as at home with long, slow simmering as it is with high speed searing or broiling. Cakes and pastries bake to perfection and, in my long experience of cooking with all materials, there is nothing better for baking pastries, tarts and quiches. It fits in perfectly with the faster pace of life we are all caught up in these days; for midweek meals, for example, a grill or skillet can produce delicious food in minutes, and served with baked potatoes or salad you cannot find a healthier alternative. But there are times when the pace slows down, and to leisurely cook a dish that takes a little longer can then be very satisfying. This may be a favorite casserole or roast, perhaps a special cake or dessert, or that pâté you have always wanted to try.

However, preparing the ingredients can be less enjoyable than the cooking so in many of my recipes the time taken to prepare ingredients is greatly assisted by the use of food processors or blenders. These take much of the tedium out of chopping, grating or making cake batters; indeed most of the cake or dessert recipes in this book are "one step" with all the ingredients being mixed as one process.

My own original pieces of Le Creuset cast iron were wedding gifts received rather more than 30 years ago, but they are still in use and maintain a bright colorful place in my kitchen among the newer shapes I now have. For the past 11 years I have acted as a consultant for Le Creuset giving guidance on technical briefs and design, writing care-and-use books with recipes, and travelling to give practical presentations and training. Once they have been shown how versatile Le Creuset cast iron pieces are, most people are amazed. They can be used on the stovetop or on the barbecue, under the broiler or in the oven and, if necessary, a piece can be moved between all of these in just one recipe. Every single piece of Le Creuset can be used on the stovetop and this includes gratin dishes or roasting dishes. Each and every stovetop can be used with ease and confidence whether gas, electric, glass-topped halogen, ceramic or the latest induction. Wood-burning stoves and even barbecues are suitable too.

Cast iron is a highly efficient material which absorbs heat very well from the stovetop. For this reason and to achieve the best cooking results, medium and low stovetop settings should be used at all times with only a few exceptions such as boiling water for pasta or vegetables. However, the use of medium and low heats does not mean that heating-up times are going to be excessively long. On the contrary, the efficiency results in heating-up times equal to, or sometimes quicker than other materials. For recipes in the oven, lower settings should also be used and if you are using one of your own recipes, always try one or two thermostat settings lower than what is normally recommended. Once a piece such as a French oven is hot, the food is surrounded by a "blanket of heat" that cools very slowly indeed. Even after you have taken a dish from the stovetop or oven, it will retain its heat and keep the food hot for some considerable time. This is especially useful for table serving. Most of the pieces are of such an attractive design, and of course color, that it is a pleasure to take them straight to the table where, with a lid in place, second helpings remain hot throughout the meal.

Color is synonymous with Le Creuset Cast Iron Cookware and the original graded flame color is recognized the world over as Le Creuset. This color symbolizes the molten iron from which each piece is made, but now a tapestry of other rich colors enables you to match your cookware to your home décor and tableware. The color is blended into the porcelain enamel (or vitreous enamel as it is also known) and is fired at a high temperature to fuse it to the cast iron. This finish converts the rather unattractive grey raw iron into a piece of cookware that is not only gorgeous to look at, but hard-wearing and rust-resistant too.

However, porcelain enamel has many other attributes and these are particularly suited to the wear-and-tear a piece encounters in the kitchen. It is said to be one of the most hygienic surfaces to cook on and, like glass (its main ingredient), bacteria do not easily grow on it. It is a solid coating, not porous, and so, unless abused, it will not stain, absorb or retain flavors and can be readily used for marinating, using acidic ingredients such as lemon juice or wine. Once a piece is cooled, left-over foods or cook-ahead meals can be stored in the refrigerator or freezer and the surface and food are unharmed. Best of all, porcelain enamel is easy to clean; my family, friends and colleagues know a pet hate of mine is cleaning up, so the easier it is the better! This is reflected in the methods which I recommend for each shape.

To talk enthusiastically about cast iron cookware and not mention the weight of the material may seem to be overlooking the fact, so the question of weight should be addressed. I have often had the question posed, "But don't you find it very heavy when you are using it day to day?" I have to answer honestly, "Yes, it is heavy", but if it were not then all its benefits for cooking and its durability would be greatly reduced. Of all the cast iron cookware produced worldwide, Le Creuset has the thinnest wall construction and this is achieved by the consistency of the manufacturing techniques used in the foundry. Interestingly, over the past 10 years or so, many cookware manufacturers have actually added weight to the bases of their cookware to make it more durable and more suitable for the high efficiency stovetops we now have. In reality the cook doesn't actually lift a piece of cookware that often. Once it is on the stovetop, it is seldom lifted or moved until taken to the table, put in the oven, or cleaned, and most shapes now have two lifting handles, so lifting is made that much easier. The weight is, and should be seen as, a strength and a real advantage for cooking. If the cast iron were too thin, the evenness of cooking and the heat-retaining properties would be greatly reduced. It would not withstand the rigors of searing and broiling and may even be distorted in shape so that it would not, over many years of use, continue to sit evenly and efficiently on the heat source.

On a personal note, I am only 5' 4" tall and, I like to think, quite petite. I use Le Creuset each and every day and probably more than most other users. I don't have huge biceps or triceps and have no intention of changing that stature! For me, the qualities the material offers far outweigh any concerns about weight. Remember, it is built to last and, with a little care, will simply go on and on producing delicious foods for years and years.

I began this introduction by suggesting that the recipes in this book would open up the repertoire of what Le Creuset Cast Iron could do for you. I hope there are some surprises in store as you use the book, such as cakes baked in French ovens, desserts made in skillets and breads baked in pâté terrine dishes. The dishes are, on the whole, cosmopolitan, and illustrate that all cuisines are well suited to the material. However, a book about French-made cookware would not be complete without some of the best-known and best-loved French recipes: Potato Dauphinois, Apple Tarté Tatin, Coq au Vin and the classic omelette are some of the simplest recipes to make, but will earn you the greatest praise.

The chapters are organized according to product shape and each chapter begins with some hints on use as well as a recipe with step-by-step photographs. A key point throughout the book is the stress laid on the use of medium or low heat for virtually all cooking. You will always be assured of good results if you follow this and other simple guidelines.

I hope you will enjoy discovering that "The Cast Iron Way to Cook" is a simple and pleasurable cooking experience, both with these new ideas and your own firm favorites. Perhaps while you cook there will be someone looking over your shoulder and that family recipe will be passed down to another generation . . . what a lovely thought.

Every piece of Le Creuset comes with full care and use instructions. These are designed to give complete information on the correct use and care of each piece, together with details of the lifetime warranty. This leaflet should therefore be read before you use the piece for the first time.

Bon Appetit!

TERMS

U.S.A.	Equivalents
All-purpose flour	Plain flour
Self-rising flour	Self-raising flour
Cornstarch	Cornflour
Semi-sweet chocolate	Plain chocolate
Superfine granulated sugar	Caster sugar
Confectioners' sugar	Icing sugar
Zucchini	Courgettes
Eggplant	Aubergine
Bell peppers	Peppers
Snow peas	Mange tout
Green beans	Haricot beans
Scallions	Spring or salad onions
Cremini mushrooms	Brown cap mushrooms
Cilantro	Coriander
Graham cracker crumbs	Digestive biscuit crumbs
Ladyfingers cookies	Sponge finger biscuits
Tomato paste	Tomato purée
Jumbo shrimp	Tiger prawns; langoustines
Ground beef	Minced beef
Monterey Jack cheese	Firm grating cheese (Cheddar)
Heavy cream	Double cream
Extra large eggs	Large eggs
Large eggs	Medium eggs
Medium eggs	Small eggs

THE MARRIAGE OF FOOD & WINE

Selecting a wine to accompany a specific dish or an entire evening meal can seem a daunting task. There are so many wines, from so many different places, made from a variety of grape types and in differing styles. How do you find that perfect bottle? By following a few basic rules, you can simplify the process and select the appropriate wine for any occasion with confidence and ease.

The first, and most important, rule to follow is quite simple. The texture and body of the wine must match the food being served. A light, delicately flavored dish requires a lighter, more delicate wine. A wine that is too powerful will obscure the nuances and subtlety of a delicate preparation and the dish will be lost. Likewise, a heavy, full-flavored dish requires a more assertive, robust wine. Always remember that wine is not meant to be standout in pairing food and wine; its role is to play second chair to the food and to enhance it.

The second rule isn't really a rule at all, but a summary of a few basic food and wine reactions. Most raw fruits, which are high in both sweetness and acidity, will make many wines taste thin, sharp and metallic. Certain vegetables, artichokes and asparagus especially, can be a problem for many wines. Most wines will again taste sharp and metallic with these vegetables. Acidic foods, usually in the form of food dressed with vinegar or citrus, decrease the perception of sourness. These foods will make wine taste richer and more mellow; if the wine is at all sweet, it will seem even more so. Sweetness in food increases our perception of sourness and astringency in wine, and makes the wine seem less sweet, stronger and less fruity. For this reason, sweets, especially chocolate, can be a problem for many wines. Remember to always pick a wine for dessert that is sweeter than the food being served.

The third rule, and the last that I will offer, is to trust your palate. There are no rights or wrongs in pairing food and wine. Food and wine pairing is very subjective and every person's sense of taste and smell is different. If you enjoy red wine with fish, that is what you should drink. Life is too short to not enjoy those combinations that suit you. Just as music and art are subjective, so is wine. So tip your glass often and enjoy what you like! Wine along with food is truly one of life's great simple pleasures.

Santé!

Mark Ray, Sommelier
Charleston Place Grill
Charleston, South Carolina

Screwpull Accessories for Wine

Before enjoying any wine, the bottle requires opening and there is no easier or better way than to use one of the exclusive Screwpull accessories.

The original table model opener was invented by a Texan wine lover and engineer, Herbert Allen, in 1979 and his invention has earned accolades worldwide ever since. The table model has now been joined by other designs, including the lever model – a must for any wine connoisseur – using the simplest of movements to remove the cork.

Today's Screwpull accessories include foil cutters, champagne stars and sommelier sets which add style, color and innovation to any wine you choose.

FRENCH OVENS – ROUND & OVAL

"French oven", "Cocotte" or "Dutch oven" are all names given to describe the same piece. It may also, in more general terms, be called a casserole dish.

Essentially, it is a sturdy cast iron cooking pot, round or oval, with a very close-fitting lid. The lid fit is important as it needs to sit so well on the rim that it forms a seal, enclosing the contents in an atmosphere of moisture that will always result in succulent well-flavored food.

Le Creuset has certainly had French ovens in its range for over 75 years and, as the book introduction relates, this shape was first produced many centuries before that. In all that time the basic design has changed little, thus endorsing the cooking qualities it provides.

Originally, its main use was to allow the long, slow cooking, either by stewing, braising or boiling, of a variety of meat, poultry, vegetables, soups and stocks. These may well have been cooked over an open fire in the kitchen or taken to a communal baker's oven where the pot could be left to simmer gently overnight in the dampened-down heat of the bread oven.

Thankfully, today, we don't have to follow that ritual and with the much greater diversity and availability of foods we can and do want to cook far more than stews or soups, as delicious as they may be on a cold day. In this respect the French oven is still the pivot of a range of cookware in a well-equipped kitchen because, as the following recipes illustrate, it can be used for a wide range of dishes: anything from savory rice to roast chicken or a mouth-watering cake.

In addition to its huge range of cooking abilities, a Le Creuset French oven has another renowned benefit – it can be taken straight from the kitchen to the table – no serving out on to another dish is necessary. The piece is elegant enough to grace any table, family or formal, and of course it keeps the food hot for serving.

The modern equipment, stovetops and ovens we use today have all become, as one would expect, more high-tech and therefore more efficient. Le Creuset cast iron is itself efficient not only in absorbing heat but, once hot, also in retaining heat. For this reason there are reminders throughout the book to use only medium or low heats for all cooking – not only for French ovens but for all other pieces as well. Just because a French oven feels heavy it doesn't mean an automatic requirement is to "blast" it with heat to get it hot. This actually works against the material and the cooking results will reflect this. Foods will stick if the piece is overheated. Foods will over-brown too quickly if the piece is overheated – but by just slowing the pace of heating to medium instead of high the heat is allowed to spread evenly and gradually throughout the material – the cook has more control and the cooking results are so much better.

Equally unhelpful is pre-heating a French oven on a high setting then, on adding the food, reducing the temperature to low. This does not save time because the heat-retaining properties of the material will not allow the piece to cool quickly and it may be necessary to move it away from the heat source to assist cooling. If it is not cooled sufficiently the same unsuccessful cooking and over-browning will result. If you already have a French oven and it is stained brown on the base and you find foods do stick, it is for no other reason than that of overheating.

Once a piece is hot on a medium setting it is usually possible to take the heat to a lower setting and still maintain the ideal cooking temperature. Being very precise about this is difficult because of the diversity of stovetops the product will meet, but if the foods and the base of the piece are beginning to brown quickly that is the sign to reduce the stovetop temperature.

All French ovens, as with the rest of the range, can be used on all types of stovetop using the guidelines just set out for them all. On glass-topped stoves, although the pieces do have enamelled bases, it is still recommended that you lift them across the surface rather than drag them.

Ovens today may be conventional electric, with radiant, fan-assisted or turbo-assisted power, or they may be gas-fired or wood-fired, but the same medium or low heat rule should be adopted with all. By doing this, you can achieve exactly the cooking rate your recipes require, remembering of course that the amount of heat the piece will retain will almost certainly allow you to use a lower cooking temperature than you may be used to with other materials. Temperatures in the oven over 400°F/200°C/Gas Mark 6 are seldom necessary, even for baking bread, and a general rule is to reduce the oven temperature you would expect to use for a recipe by at least one or more settings. Therefore, if a recipe calls for 375°F/190°C/Gas Mark 5, try 350°F/180°C/Gas Mark 4 or even 325°F/160°C/Gas Mark 3.

The cooking efficiency of a cast iron French oven is best illustrated by the recipe for Simple Vegetable and Saffron Rice on page 20. Here the ingredients are prepared on the stovetop, brought to the boil, then, with the lid in place, left for just two minutes at a simmer to allow the heat to spread evenly throughout the whole piece, including the lid. When the whole thing is hot, it is moved away from the heat, allowing the rice to finish cooking in the retained heat the pot provides. For those who have little success with cooking rice, this is exceptionally reliable and the heat of the cast iron 20 minutes after being removed from the heat source is quite a surprise.

In a completely different way, the heat-retaining qualities can be used in reverse to keep foods cold. If you are having a party and need to hold quantities of ice cream or crushed ice, a French oven, once chilled, will keep its contents cold for some considerable time.

Roasting in a French oven uses a dry technique for cooking, adding no liquid at all during the cooking period other than a little oil or butter for greasing. Chicken, capon, a small turkey or even game birds are all particularly suited to this method of cooking as the flesh remains very moist, while the skin becomes golden brown and crisp. Pork, beef and lamb are also very good but they do not crisp on the outside as they would with open roasting. However, if it's succulence you want, the method is very successful. A big plus after roasting is that while the meat is resting prior to carving the cooking residues left in the French oven can be used on the stovetop to make a well-flavored sauce or gravy and, of course, there is only one pot to clean. Tarragon Roasted Chicken on page 17 will take you through the method. The maximum oven roasting temperature you should require for any meats is 350°F/180°C/Gas Mark 4, allowing, very approximately, the same times you would use for open roasting. After cooking, you can check that it's done with a meat thermometer. An oval French oven is the ideal shape for roasting.

The round 2¾ quart (20 cm), 3½ quart (22 cm) and 4½ quart (24 cm) French ovens all have the same diameter as regular cake molds. There is no reason why a cake cannot be baked in any one of these pieces. For general ease of release, lining the French oven with greaseproof baking parchment or a pre-formed cake liner is advisable. The recipe on page 25 for the Double Chocolate Marbled Pound Cake is sure to be a winner with your family. After baking and cooling, the cake can be stored in the French oven, and the lid seal is so good you have the perfect storage container.

But to return the French oven to its roots, it is unsurpassed in its ability to cook anything from a spicy chili in 30 minutes to a hotpot in 5 hours with the same reliable succulence and flavor for either. A French oven comes in a range of sizes – from a diminutive round 2 quart (18 cm) to the giant oval 9½ quart (35 cm) – so there is a size and shape for all needs and all functions.

The following general tips will help you to choose and use French ovens. The first recipe, Beef 'n' Beer, takes you through a "step-by-step" guide with photographs and the principles here can then be adapted to suit a number of your own recipes. The remaining recipes in this chapter give ideas for the wide variety of uses for French ovens and you will undoubtedly be able to provide a few more.

General Tips

● Choose a size to suit your everyday needs. This may sound odd, but for best results a French oven should be at least half, or better still, three-quarters full with food and liquid. It is not ideal to purchase a very large pot for an occasional family gathering if there are usually only 2 or 4 people to serve. A small amount of food in a large French oven will cook more quickly and is more likely to become dry.
● It is difficult to generalize about sizes to suit each family's requirements as appetites vary so greatly. However, as a very approximate guide, a round 3½ quart (22 cm) will cook most recipes to serve 4; the 4½ quart (24 cm) to serve 6; and the 5½ quart (26 cm) to serve 8.
● If you believe you will use the French oven more for roasting than for casseroles or braises, choose the oval shape as poultry and joints sit better in this shape.
● If you prefer a stew or casserole to have a deeper brown color, cook it inside the oven where the all-round heat of the piece will give greater caramelization of the ingredients and liquid. If this is not important, most recipes can be simmered on the stovetop where the same degree of tenderness and succulence will still be achieved.
● Do not use high heats unless the French oven is simply being used to boil water or reduce stocks. Medium and low heats should be used at all times on the stovetop and in the oven.
● Where possible, always add hot liquid to a hot pot, not cold liquid to a hot pot. If adding cold liquid is unavoidable, for example if wine is being used, move the piece away from the heat source for a few moments then pour in the liquid slowly.

- Generally, it is better to use plastic, wooden or Le Creuset heat-resistant silicone spoons and spatulas for stirring. These will not scratch or damage the porcelain enamel surface. However, occasional use of metal tools or spoons may be necessary and is acceptable. If metal marks are left on the porcelain enamel surface these can be removed with Le Creuset cookware cleaner.
- Do not, however, use electric hand-held mixer blades on the porcelain enamel surface, or bang metal spoons or blades on the top rim of the piece. Repeated abuse in this way will eventually damage the porcelain enamel causing tiny flaws that may give way to rust.
- The upturned lid of a French oven can be used as a holding dish for ingredients either after they are prepared, or after pre-browning. Take care, however, not to place the upturned lid over a hot heat source as the lifting knob will be permanently damaged.
- The lifting knob on the lid of French ovens is oven heat resistant to 400°F/ 200°C/Gas Mark 6 but do not allow it to come into direct contact with a naked flame or the hot elements of a broiler or an oven.
- When used on the stovetop, all French oven side-lifting handles will become hot, therefore, always have a dry cloth or oven mitts ready for lifting.
- After cooking, a hot French oven should not be filled with, or plunged into, cold water as damage to the porcelain enamel may occur. To clean effectively and easily, leave the piece to stand for 3 to 5 minutes, then fill with warm water. Leave again for a further 10 to 15 minutes before washing in hot soapy water, rinsing and drying thoroughly. In this way any residues on the surface will wash away easily, or can be lightly scoured off with a nylon cleaning pad.
- The porcelain enamel will retain its new appearance if polished occasionally with the special Le Creuset cookware cleaner.

BEEF 'N' BEER

Serves 6
Preparation time: 20 minutes
Cooking time: 3½ to 4 hours

Cooking meat in beer or ale is a centuries-old cooking technique, and the flavor harmonizes with beef particularly well. This is a fairly rustic recipe that makes a good winter weekend meal or a casual entertaining dish. This recipe can be cooked in any round or oval 4½ to 5-quart (24 to 29 cm) French oven.

3 tablespoons vegetable oil
2 large onions, sliced thinly
2 garlic cloves, sliced thinly
3 cups (450 g) thickly sliced carrots
2 to 2½ pounds (1 to 1.2 kg) beef
    chuck, in 2-inch (5 cm) chunks
a few sprigs of fresh thyme,
    parsley and rosemary
2 bay leaves
3 cups (750 ml) ale or beer
    (see Cook's Tips, below)
salt and freshly ground black
    pepper

For the bread topping:
twelve 1-inch (2.5 cm) thick slices
    from a French baguette
2 tablespoons Dijon mustard
1 tablespoon fresh chopped
    parsley

1 Heat the oil in the French oven over a medium heat on the stovetop. Add the onions, garlic, and carrots and fry just until they begin to color. Use a slotted spoon to remove them. Use the upturned lid as a holding plate.

2 Add the beef in two batches and brown evenly. Remove the pan from the heat.

3 Preheat the oven to 275°F/140°C/Gas Mark 1. Return all the browned ingredients to the pan. Add the herbs, tied together to make a bouquet garni, with the beer, seasoning, and ½ cup (125 ml) water.

Stir together, cover, and cook in the oven for 3 to 3½ hours until the beef is very tender.

4 Spread one side of each bread slice with the mustard. When the beef is tender check the liquid level, which should be just covering the meat. Add a little more beer, if necessary, and remove the bouquet garni.

5 Push the bread, mustard side up, into the top of the liquid, squeezing the slices tightly together.

Return, uncovered, to the oven for 20 minutes longer to lightly color and crisp the bread. Sprinkle with the chopped parsley.

If it suits your schedule better, the beef can be cooked at a lower temperature for a longer time, such as 225°F/110°C/ Gas Mark ¼ for 5 to 6 hours.

For the beer in this recipe use pale ale, or lager if ale is not available. Guinness from Ireland also works well.

MUSSELS WITH CHILI-CREAM SAUCE

Serves 4 as an appetizer, or 2 or 3 as a main course

Preparation time: 20 minutes

Cooking time: 10 minutes

The heat which the chili brings to this cream sauce goes very well with the mussels. This can be a very casual meal, or an appetizer for a dinner party. Make sure you provide bowls for the empty shells. The recipe uses a round 5½-quart (26 cm) French oven.

4 pounds 8 ounces (2 kg) fresh mussels, cleaned (see Cook's Tips, below)

1 cup (250 ml) dry white wine

2 shallots, chopped finely

1 chili, seeded and chopped finely

1 large garlic clove, chopped finely

a few sprigs of flat-leaf parsley

For the sauce:

½ cup (125 ml) low-fat whipping cream

1 tablespoon cornstarch

2 tablespoons fresh chopped flat-leaf parsley

a little coarse salt and freshly ground black pepper

crusty bread, to serve

1 Put the cleaned mussels into the French oven with the wine, shallots, chili, garlic, and parsley. Stir together. Cover and bring to a boil. Reduce the heat and cook steadily for 3 to 4 minutes until the mussels are cooked and open.

2 Tip the mussels into a large colander set over a bowl to catch the cooking liquid; reserve the liquid for the sauce. Discard any mussels that have not opened.

3 Carefully tip the cooking liquid back into the French oven, but do not use the final drop because it can contain grit or sand from the mussels.

4 Bring the cooking liquid to a boil and leave to boil for 3 to 4 minutes to concentrate the flavor. Blend the cornstarch with the cream and stir this into the cooking liquid, together with the parsley and seasoning to taste.

5 When the sauce has thickened, tip the mussels back into the French oven and stir so a little goes into each shell. Serve immediately from the French oven with crusty bread to soak up the sauce.

This recipe can also be cooked in the oval 5-quart (29 cm) French oven.

Always store mussels in the refrigerator and cook within 24 hours of purchase. Rinse them well in plenty of cold water, pulling out any beards and scraping off barnacles. Discard any mussels that are damaged or gaping open and do not close after rinsing and handling. After cooking, discard any mussels that did not open.

COMFORT CHICKEN

Serves 6
Preparation time: 15 minutes
Cooking time: about 3 hours

This really is a comfort meal, all cooked in one pot so there is minimal clean up too. This recipe uses the round 4½-quart (24 cm) French oven.

2 tablespoons vegetable oil

1 large onion, sliced thinly

4 celery stalks, chopped into
 1-inch (2.5 cm) pieces

4 large carrots, cut into ½-inch
 (1 cm) slices

2 medium leeks, cut into
 1-inch (2.5 cm) slices

6 boned and skinned chicken
 breast halves

3¼ cups (225 g) thickly sliced
 cremini mushrooms

2 tablespoons fresh chopped
 parsley

2½ cups (625 ml) hot chicken
 stock

½ cup (125 ml) low-fat whipping
 cream

2 pounds 4 ounces (1 kg) boiling
 potatoes, cut into ¼-inch (5 mm)
 slices

1 tablespoon (15 g) butter,
 softened

1 Heat the oil in the French oven over a medium heat on the stovetop. Add the onion, celery, carrots, and leeks and fry until these just begin to brown. Use a slotted spoon to lift out the vegetables, draining them well; use the upturned lid as a holding dish.

2 Add the chicken pieces to the oil remaining in the French oven and brown evenly on all sides, working in batches if necessary. As each piece of chicken is browned, remove it and drain off any excess oil or fat.

3 Preheat the oven to 275°F/140°/Gas Mark 1. Remove the French oven from the heat. Put half the vegetables into the bottom and cover with 3 chicken pieces. Add the mushrooms in a thick layer, together with half the chopped parsley and some seasoning. Repeat these layers with the remaining vegetables and chicken, scattering the last of the parsley on top with more seasoning. Pour in the hot stock and cream. (Always add hot stock to a hot pan.)

4 Arrange closely overlapping potato slices over the chicken pieces, brush with the butter, and season lightly. Cover with the lid and cook in the heated oven for 2½ to 3 hours. Uncover for the last 20 minutes to brown the potato topping.

 This recipe can also be cooked in an oval 3½-quart (25 cm) French oven.

 If you prefer, cook this recipe at a higher oven temperature for a shorter time, such as 300°F/150°C/Gas Mark 2, for 1½ to 2 hours.

Boneless beef or pork, cut into 1-inch (2.5 cm) cubes, can also be cooked using this recipe and method. Cook for 1 hour longer than the time given in the main recipe.

TARRAGON ROASTED CHICKEN

Serves 6 to 8

Preparation time: 5 minutes

Cooking time: 2 to 2½ hours

You might never have considered the possibility of using a covered French oven as a roasting pan, but it works exceptionally well, producing a moist, succulent bird with a golden, crisp skin. While the chicken is resting before being carved, the French oven bottom can be used on the stovetop to make a delicious tarragon-flavored cream sauce. An oval 5-quart (29 cm) French oven is the ideal piece for this recipe.

a little vegetable oil, for greasing
4½ pound (2 kg) roasting chicken
1 tablespoon dried tarragon
salt and freshly ground black
   pepper

For the sauce:

2 cups (500 ml) hot chicken stock
½ cup (125 ml) heavy cream
1 tablespoon dried tarragon
2 teaspoons cornstarch

1 Preheat the oven to 350°F/180°C/Gas Mark 4. Lightly grease the inside of the French oven. Wash and dry the chicken and truss into shape. Grease it lightly all over with vegetable oil and rub a little salt and pepper into the skin. Place the chicken breast side up in the French oven and sprinkle the tarragon over the breast and legs.

2 Cover the pan with the lid, place it in the heated oven, and roast for 2 to 2½ hours until the juices run clear, not pink, when the thigh is pierced with a skewer, or an instant-read thermometer reads 180°F (82°C).

3 Lift out the chicken, cover it with aluminum foil and a clean dish towel, and leave to rest for 10 to 15 minutes while making the sauce.

4 To make the sauce, pour out any excess fat from the French oven. Pour the hot stock into the pan and place it over medium heat on the stovetop and bring to a boil. Stir to remove any residues from the bottom, which can be incorporated into the sauce. Once the liquid is boiling, stir in the cream blended with the tarragon and cornstarch. Reduce the heat and simmer for 2 to 3 minutes, stirring.

5 Taste and adjust the seasoning of the sauce before serving it with the carved chicken.

 This recipe can also be cooked in a round 5½-quart (26 cm) French oven.

 This method of roasting also works very well with pork and beef. Use the same oven temperature as above and check it is done with a meat thermometer or your usual method.

 A medium-bodied Chardonnay from Australia or from the Napa Valley will work well with this dish. For those who prefer red, try Beaujolais.

COQ AU VIN

Serves 8 to 10
Preparation time: 25 minutes
Cooking time: about 3 hours

There are many versions of this classic French dish, most cooked in a full-bodied red wine. However the main ingredient is always the cockerel which has, hopefully, lived its life scratching around the farm and fields before joining the pot. Few of us, unfortunately, have access to these full-flavored birds, but always use a good-quality chicken. This recipe uses an oval ..5-quart (29 cm) French oven.

2 tablespoons extra-virgin olive oil
2 cups (225 g) chopped bacon
1 medium onion, chopped
two 4½ pound (2 kg) chickens, each cut into 8 pieces
5 tablespoons brandy
a few sprigs of fresh thyme, rosemary and parsley
2 bay leaves
3 garlic cloves, crushed
1 tablespoon tomato paste
1 tablespoon lemon juice
1 tablespoon sugar
1 bottle (75 cl) full-bodied, dry red wine (see Wine Tip)
2 tablespoons chopped fresh flat-leaf parsley, to garnish

For the glazed shallots and mushrooms:
1 tablespoon (15 g) butter
2 tablespoons olive oil
12 ounces (350 g) shallots
12 ounces (350 g) button mushrooms, cleaned

For the beurre manié:
2 tablespoons (30 g) butter, softened
2 tablespoons all-purpose flour

1 Heat the oil in the French oven over medium heat on the stovetop. Add the bacon and onion and cook, stirring, until both are softened and then remove, draining well.

2 Fry the chicken in batches until all the pieces are evenly browned, then return them all to the pan with the bacon and onion. Remove the French oven from the heat and add the brandy. Carefully ignite, standing well back until the flames subside, then return the pan to the heat.

3 Preheat the oven to 275°F/140°C/Gas Mark 1. Tie all the herbs into a bundle with fine string and add this to the French oven with the garlic, tomato paste, lemon juice, sugar and red wine. Cover with the lid and cook in the oven for 2 to 2½ hours until the chicken is very tender.

4 About 30 minutes before the chicken finishes cooking, melt the butter and oil in a large skillet over medium heat. Add the shallots and fry for 10 to 15 minutes until they are golden brown and soft; transfer to a plate. Add the mushrooms to the pan and toss so they are just cooked and colored.

5 Blend the butter and flour together in a small bowl. Remove a few pieces of the cooked chicken from the French oven to make room to stir in the beurre manié. Add this in small amounts, stirring after each addition so that the sauce remains smooth.

6 When all the beurre manié has been incorporated, return the chicken together with the shallots and mushrooms. Simmer for 2 to 3 minutes. Sprinkle the top generously with the parsley and serve from the French oven.

 This recipe can also be cooked in a round 5½-quart (26 cm) French oven.

 If a lower fat content is a requirement, remove the chicken skin before cooking and thicken the cooking liquid with 2 teaspoons blended cornstarch instead of the beurre manié.

 This dish has traditionally been prepared with red Burgundy which makes an excellent accompaniment to the meal: try one of the red wines from the Burgundy villages of Marsannay or Santenay. Or try a Pinot Noir from Oregon.

SIMPLE VEGETABLE AND SAFFRON RICE

Serves 6 to 8
Preparation time: 10 minutes
Cooking time: 20 minutes

As the title suggests this is the simplest way to cook a vegetable rice dish. The heat-retaining qualities of the cast iron are so good that once the French oven is hot it can be removed from the stovetop and left for the rice to continue cooking with no additional bottom heat. Just a stir at the end of the 20-minute cooking period and the rice will be ready to serve. But don't be tempted to peep inside while it is standing, or some of the heat will be lost. A round 3½-quart (22 cm) French oven is ideal for this recipe.

2 tablespoons (30 g) butter,
    softened
1 medium onion, chopped
1 medium bell pepper, seeded
    and chopped
1 cup (175 g) canned whole corn
    kernels, drained
1¾ cups (350 g) instant long-grain
    rice
3 cups (750 ml) hot chicken stock
¼ teaspoon saffron powder
1 tablespoon fresh chopped cilantro
1 teaspoon salt
freshly ground black pepper
1 cup (225 g) cooked shrimp,
    flaked tuna or salmon (optional)

1 Melt the butter in the French oven over medium heat on the stovetop. Add the onion and the bell pepper and fry gently, without coloring, for 2 to 3 minutes.

2 Stir in the corn kernels, rice, hot stock, saffron, cilantro, and the seasonings. Stir well and bring to a slow boil.

3 Cover with the lid, reduce the heat to low, and simmer for 2 minutes.

4 Remove the pan from the heat and leave to stand for 20 minutes: do not remove the lid during the standing time. Stir well before serving.

To make a more substantial main course, add the cooked shrimp, tuna or salmon and return to the heat for 2 to 3 minutes to ensure the seafood is thoroughly heated.

This recipe can also be cooked in a 3½-quart (30 cm) buffet casserole.

Vegetable stock can be used instead of chicken stock.
    Instead of saffron, you can use 1 teaspoon ground turmeric to give the rice a rich, golden color.

This rice dish also makes a good salad dish. Leave it to cool then stir in 2 tablespoons French vinaigrette dressing.

PHEASANT IN MADEIRA SAUCE

Serves 4
Preparation time: 15 minutes
Cooking time: about 3 hours

*Pheasants contain considerably
less fat pound for pound than
chicken, so like other game birds
they are a good addition to a low-
fat diet. However, they need careful
cooking to avoid becoming dry and
stringy. Over the years I have tried a
variety of methods, but this slow
cooking in Madeira wine is by far
the best. An oval 5-quart (29 cm)
French oven is ideal for this recipe.*

2 tablespoons vegetable oil
1 cup (125 g) chopped bacon
12 shallots
two 2¼ pound (1 kg) pheasants
8 ounces (225 g) button
    mushrooms
2 bay leaves
4 sprigs of fresh thyme
1½ cups (375 ml) Madeira wine
1 cup (250 ml) hot chicken stock
2 teaspoons (10 g) butter,
    softened
2 teaspoons all-purpose flour
salt and freshly ground black pepper
a few sprigs of fresh thyme, to
    garnish

1 Make sure the pheasants
are free of feathers and shot
pellets. Truss with string.

2 Heat the oil in the French
oven over medium heat on the
stovetop. Add the bacon and
shallots and fry for just a few
minutes, stirring.

3 Preheat the oven to
275°F/140°C/Gas Mark 1. Add
one pheasant at a time to the
French oven and brown all over in
the hot oil. Lift out and set aside
the first one before adding the
second so there is enough room to
turn the bird over.

4 When both pheasants are
brown, return them to the pan with
the button mushrooms, bay
leaves, thyme, Madeira, half the
hot chicken stock, and seasoning.
Cover and transfer to the heated
oven for 2½ to 3 hours until the
meat is cooked through and very
tender.

5 Transfer the pheasants to a
warm serving platter, cover with
aluminum foil and a clean dish
towel, and set aside to rest while

making the sauce. Remove the
thyme stems from the cooking
liquid.

6 Put the French oven on the
stovetop and reboil the cooking
liquid, adding the remaining stock.
Blend together the butter and flour
to form a beurre manié. Drop small
amounts into the liquid, stirring so
the sauce remains smooth.
Continue simmering until the sauce
thickens, then taste and adjust the
seasoning.

7 Cut each pheasant in half
and serve with a little of the sauce
poured over the top. Garnish with
a few tiny sprigs of fresh thyme.

 *This recipe can also be
cooked in a round 5½-quart
(26 cm) French oven.*

 *Madeira wine is a fortified wine
produced on a Portuguese
island of the same name. If you
don't have any, use a medium-
sweet sherry instead.*
    *Guinea fowl or Cornish hens
can also be used for this recipe.*

 *Red Burgundy is always a good
bet with pheasant but a more
fruit-driven California Pinot Noir
from Carneros or the Russian
River Valley would be the first
choice. A Sercial or Verdecho
Madeira is an interesting and
unusual option.*

BEAN FEAST

Serves 8 to 12

Preparation time: 15 minutes + soaking the beans

Cooking time: 1 to 1½ hours for the beans, 45 to 50 minutes for the rest of the recipe

This is a very versatile bean recipe. It can be cooked and eaten the same day, or, as with so many dishes, it can be made ahead and reheated, which allows the flavors to really infuse and improve. Any selection of beans can be used, and if time is short, canned beans are good substitutes. This recipe uses a round 4½-quart (24 cm) French oven.

1 cup (175 g) small dry white beans

1 cup (175 g) dry red kidney beans

4 tablespoons extra-virgin olive oil

1 large red onion, chopped coarsely

3 large carrots, cut into ¼-inch (5 mm) slices

3 celery stalks, cut into ¼-inch (5 mm) slices

2 potatoes, cut into ½-inch (1 cm) dice

1 pound (450 g) canned crushed tomatoes

2 teaspoons tomato paste

1 teaspoon caraway seeds

1 teaspoon dried thyme

1 teaspoon paprika

1 cup (125 g) thin green beans, cut into ½-inch (1 cm) pieces

2 cups (225 g) cauliflower florets, broken into small pieces

2 tablespoons fresh chopped flat-leaf parsley

salt and freshly ground black pepper

boiled brown rice or pasta, to serve (optional)

1 Put the white and red beans into the French oven, cover with cold water, and leave to soak overnight. The next day, discard the soaking water. Re-cover the beans with fresh water and place the pan over high heat on the stovetop. Bring to a boil and boil gently for 1 to 1½ hours until the beans are tender. Leave the beans to cool completely in the cooking liquid, then drain, reserving 1½ cups (375 ml) of the liquid.

2 Rinse and dry the French oven. Heat the oil in it over medium heat on the stovetop. Add the onions, carrots, celery, and potatoes and cook until they begin to soften and color, stirring occasionally.

3 Add the crushed tomatoes with their juice, tomato paste, caraway seeds, thyme, and paprika. Return the beans to the French oven with the reserved cooking liquid and a little salt and pepper.

4 Cover with the lid and simmer for 30 to 40 minutes, or until the vegetables are tender. Add the green beans and cauliflower and continue simmering for 15 minutes longer. Stir in the parsley and adjust the seasoning to taste.

5 Serve as a side vegetable or as a main course with boiled brown rice or pasta.

 This recipe can also be cooked in any other large round or oval French oven.

 Do not add salt when cooking the beans in Step 1. Salt will toughen the skins and prevent them from cooking evenly.

CHARLESTON GUMBO

Serves 6
Preparation time: 20 minutes
Cooking time: 1 to 1½ hours

This spicy, thick "soup" is traditionally thickened with a roux of flour and oil. In this version, the addition of a little potato with the okra does the thickening as the gumbo cooks, so the roux is eliminated. Cook the clams within 24 hours of purchase, and discard any open ones that do not close when tapped. Serve with long-grain rice. This recipe uses a round 5½-quart (26 cm) French oven.

1 cup (125 g) chopped bacon
2 tablespoons olive oil
1 red onion, chopped
4 celery stalks, chopped
1 green bell pepper, seeded and
    chopped
2 garlic cloves, chopped finely
2 small red chilies, seeded and
    chopped
4 cups (500 g) peeled and
    chopped tomatoes
3 cups (500 g) new potatoes, cut
    into ½-inch (1 cm) dice
heaping 1 cup (225 g) okra, cut
    into ½-inch (1 cm) slices

a pinch of cayenne pepper
¼ teaspoon ground turmeric
2 good sprigs of fresh thyme
4 cups (1 litre) fish stock or water
¼ teaspoon coarse sea salt
1 pound (450 g) cod fillet, cut into
    2½-inch (6 cm) pieces
2¼ pounds (1 kg) large raw shrimp
2¼ pounds (1 kg) small raw clams
2 tablespoons fresh chopped
    parsley, to garnish

1 Place the French oven over a medium heat setting on the stovetop and add the bacon. Cook, stirring, until the fat begins to run. Add the olive oil with the onion, celery, bell pepper, garlic, and chilies. Reduce the heat to low and cook these vegetables until they begin to soften.

2 Add the tomatoes and all the remaining ingredients, except the seafood.

3 Cover and simmer for 45 minutes to 1 hour until the vegetables are very tender. Add all the seafood, stirring well. Cover again and cook for 5 to 8 minutes longer until the cod is cooked and

the clams are open; discard any clams that remain closed.

4 Just before serving, stir in the chopped parsley and check the seasoning. Ladle over the cooked long-grain rice.

This recipe can also be made in the oval 5-quart (29 cm) French oven, or Bouillabaisse pot.

Flounder, bass fillets or monkfish can also be used.
If you have time to make your own fish stock, it really adds to the overall flavor. Simmer together a few shrimp

shells with one diced carrot, one chopped celery stalk, a few sprigs of parsley and thyme and one bay leaf with 4 cups (1 litre) water for 1 hour. Strain before use.

ZUCCHINI SOUP WITH CURRIED BREAD FINGERS

Serves 6

Preparation time: 20 minutes

Cooking time: 45 minutes for the soup, 5 minutes for the bread fingers

These curried bread fingers go very well with this light soup. If your family does not like curry flavor, omit the curry powder and dust the tops with a little paprika. This recipe uses a round 4½-quart (24 cm) French oven.

2 tablespoons olive oil

2¼ pounds (1 kg) zucchini, cut into 1-inch (2.5 cm) slices

1 medium onion, chopped

2 floury potatoes, cut into ½-inch (1 cm) dice

4 cups (1 litre) hot chicken stock, plus a little extra for serving, if necessary

1 teaspoon dried marjoram

1 teaspoon salt

¼ teaspoon freshly ground black pepper

For the curried bread fingers:

6 thick slices white bread, crusts removed

1 tablespoon (15 g) butter, softened

3 tablespoons mayonnaise

1½ teaspoons medium curry powder

½ cup (60 g) finely grated Monterey Jack cheese

a little salt and freshly ground black pepper

1 Heat the oil in the French oven over a medium heat on the stovetop. Add the zucchini, onion, and potatoes and cook, stirring occasionally, for 3 to 4 minutes.

2 Add the hot stock with the marjoram and seasonings. Stir well, cover, and simmer over low heat for 40 to 45 minutes, until the vegetables are very tender.

3 While the soup is cooking, prepare the curried bread fingers. Toast the bread on one side only under a hot broiler. Mix together all the other ingredients and divide between the 6 slices of bread, spreading it onto the untoasted sides. Place the slices on a cookie sheet and chill, if possible, for 30 minutes.

4 Remove the soup from the heat and leave the vegetables to cool, uncovered, for 15 minutes. Purée the soup in a food processor or blender, return to the French oven, and reheat before serving, adjusting the consistency with a little extra stock if necessary.

5 While the soup is re-heating, place the bread slices under a hot broiler and broil until golden brown. Cut each slice into 3 fingers and serve warm with the soup.

 This recipe can also be cooked in a 5-quart (29 cm) French oven..

 This soup freezes well for up to one month. Make the soup up to step 4 and then purée the soup. Cool and freeze. Adjust the consistency when re-heating.

 If the soup is being served as a first course, try a Champagne or Sparkling wine with it.

DOUBLE CHOCOLATE MARBLED POUND CAKE

Makes 16 slices

Preparation time: 15 minutes

Cooking time: 1 to 1¼ hours

This cake is very moist and has two surprises in store. First, a mixture of chocolate and vanilla marbled together that will vary every time it is baked, and, second, the pleasure of biting into the chocolate marbling only to discover the extra-gooey chocolate pockets! This pound cake recipe bakes beautifully in a round 2¾-quart (20 cm) French oven.

2 sticks (225 g) butter, softened

1 cup (225 g) superfine granulated sugar

3 large eggs

½ cup (125 ml) sour cream

2 teaspoons vanilla extract

2¼ cups (300 g) self-rising flour, sifted

2 tablespoons unsweetened cocoa powder

⅓ cup (60 g) baking chocolate chips

1 Preheat the oven to 300°F/150°C/Gas Mark 2. Grease and dust the inside of the French oven with flour.

2 Cream the butter and sugar together until light and fluffy. Beat together the eggs, sour cream, and vanilla extract and gradually add this mixture to the creamed mixture, beating well between additions.

3 Using a large metal spoon, fold in the sifted flour a little at a time. When all the flour has been added, transfer one quarter of the batter to another bowl.

4 Fold the cocoa powder and chocolate chips into the smaller amount of batter.

5 Put half the vanilla batter into the French oven and level the surface. Add the chocolate batter in 3 large spoonfuls, spacing them apart. Spread the remaining vanilla batter on top.

6 Using a knife, make 3 or 4 wide swirling movements to create

the marbling effect; do not make many more swirls, or the definition of the marble will be reduced.

7 Level the top of the batter and make a small dip about 2 inches (5 cm) wide in the middle to help keep the cake top level while it rises as it bakes.

8 Bake the cake just below the middle of the oven for 1 to 1¼ hours until the top is golden brown and just firm to the touch. When the cake is baked through, a turkey skewer or toothpick inserted into the middle will come out clean. Leave the cake to cool in the French oven for at least 15 minutes before unmolding it on to a cake cooling rack. Cool thoroughly before storing in the clean cold dish or an airtight container. It will keep for 1 or 2 weeks.

Low-fat soft margarine can be used instead of the butter in this recipe.

Steps 1 and 2 can also be done by putting all the ingredients in a food processor and adding 1 teaspoon baking powder to the flour.

The baking powder adds extra aeration to the batter which the processor alone cannot do.

BUFFET CASSEROLES

Perhaps I shouldn't have a favorite piece of Le Creuset, but I'm afraid I do: the buffet casserole. When I began work as a consultant for Le Creuset it was one of my first new pieces and the original 3½ quart (30 cm) and now a newer 2½ quart (26cm) are in constant use.

It may be easier to say what the buffet casserole is less useful for, rather than what it is excellent for, but I will take the less easy option and extol its advantages.

The base, on its own, can be used as a frypan or sauté pan (using the lid if you need to steam-fry at any time). The base is also a good-size dish for gratins, or perhaps recipes finished with a potato topping. The depth of the base is such that it allows it to be slid under most broilers to crisp or brown a topping. It is also an excellent shape to use for family-size cobbler or crumble recipes, either sweet or savory, giving ample depth for the filling and plenty of space for the biscuit cobbler to brown evenly. Cakes, desserts and pies with either a pastry or biscuit crust will bake very evenly and have the added virtue of being cooked at lower temperatures.

Rice dishes such as a pilau, risotto or paella suit the wide shape, which gives ample space for the rice to expand and be stirred as it cooks. This chapter includes a recipe for risotto, using a mixture of dried wild and fresh mushrooms (see page 30). Risotto is a recipe that needs gentle simmering to allow the Italian arborio rice to slowly expand and absorb the flavors of the wine, stock and other flavorings you may add, and this can be achieved extremely well in the buffet casserole.

Pasta sauces are a must in most homes these days. Young and old alike enjoy the wide range of flavors you can prepare. A sauce can be made in the buffet casserole base, then have the pasta stirred through it. Alternatively, the pasta can be cooked in the buffet casserole itself, drained and returned to the hot dish with the sauce poured on top; immediately you have the perfect "cook 'n' serve" pasta dish.

The poaching of fish, chicken, fruits or vegetables has long been recognized as a way of retaining the flavor, moisture and shape of the food. It did suffer a decline some years ago but is now back in fashion, not least because of the nutritional benefits it can bring. It is an extremely good cooking method for those people who have restricted or low-fat diets, but the overall benefits can be enjoyed by everyone. There is no competition when it comes to gently poaching a piece of freshly-caught salmon in a little white wine, herbs and a touch of lemon (see page 34). Served hot or cold, the flesh will always be succulent and full of its natural flavors. Chicken for salads remains very moist and plump when it is poached rather than roasted or baked. Traditionally, poaching means covering the food completely in liquid, but by using the buffet casserole, with its well-fitting lid, the food can be cooked in far less liquid while still being bathed in moisture. The wide shallow shape makes the handling of the food so much easier too.

Stir-frying, or the slow roasting of small Cornish hens, poussins, pork chops or ribs are also excellent. For those days when you simply want to pour a jar of sauce over some chicken breasts, the buffet casserole, when you take its elegance to the table, will imply that you have taken so much more time and trouble!

But finally, of course, the buffet casserole, like the French oven, can be used as a traditional casserole dish for the long, slow simmering of ragoûts and braises, using it to seal and brown ingredients on the stovetop before transferring it to the oven. All the general tips given on pages 12 and 13 for French ovens apply equally to the buffet casserole, particularly the use of medium and low heats for all cooking, so please refer to these pages for more information.

There are just two sizes of buffet casserole, the 3½ quart (30 cm) and the 2½ quart (26 cm). The larger size will cater for approximately 6 people and the smaller one for 4.

PORK MEDALLIONS WITH CREAM AND MUSTARD SAUCE

Serves 6
Preparation time: 10 minutes
Cooking time: 15 minutes

This is an ideal dish for entertaining as it can be completely cooked about an hour ahead, then covered with the lid to keep it moist. Reheat gently when the guests arrive. This recipe is cooked in the 2½-quart (26 cm) buffet casserole.

2¼ pounds (1 kg) pork tenderloin
2 teaspoons olive oil
1 tablespoon butter
2 shallots, chopped finely
1 cup (125 g) small porcini mushrooms
⅓ cup (80 ml) dry white wine
1 cup (250 ml) heavy cream
2 teaspoons Dijon mustard
salt and freshly ground black pepper

To serve:
boiled baby new potoates, noodles or rice
a green vegetable or mixed green leaf salad

1 Trim the tenderloin of any fat and tendons. Cut into 1½-inch (4 cm) thick slices. Put these between pieces of plastic wrap and beat out until ½-inch (1 cm) thick; season lightly.

2 Heat the oil and butter in the buffet casserole over medium heat. Add the shallots and fry until soft, but not brown. Add a few pork medallions at a time and fry for 2 to 3 minutes on each side. Lift out the pork as each piece is ready and keep hot on the upturned lid. Continue frying until all the pork pieces are cooked. Add the mushrooms and fry for 2 minutes and then remove from the pan.

3 Remove the buffet casserole from the heat and deglaze the pan with the white wine. Stir in the cream and mustard. Return the buffet casserole to a medium heat and simmer until the sauce bubbles and thickens slightly.

4 Put the medallions and mushrooms back into the sauce and thoroughly reheat, adjusting the seasoning.

Serve with boiled baby new potatoes, noodles or rice, and a green vegetable or mixed green leaf salad.

 This recipe can also be cooked in a 10½-inch (26 cm) iron-handle skillet or frypan.

 Low-fat whipping cream can be used for the sauce.

 A full-bodied, rich Chardonnay from California or Australia will work beautifully with the pork.

VEGETABLE CASSEROLE WITH CRISPY TOPPING

Serves 4 to 6 as a main course, or 6 to 8 as a side vegetable dish

Preparation time: 20 minutes

Cooking time: 1½ hours

The wide shape of the buffet casserole lends itself perfectly to the type of recipe that is finished under the broiler to produce a crisp topping. The vegetables can be cooked in advance and then reheated and finished with the crisp topping just before you serve. This recipe uses the 3½-quart (30 cm) buffet casserole.

4 tablespoons olive oil

1 large red onion, chopped roughly

1 pound (450 g) butternut squash, peeled and cut into ½-inch (1 cm) dice

1 pound (450 g) eggplant, cut into ½-inch (1 cm) dice

4 celery stalks, cut into ¼-inch (5 mm) slices

4 zucchini, cut into ½-inch (1 cm) slices

1 pound (450 g) canned crushed tomatoes with their juice

12 fresh basil leaves

2 tablespoons chopped fresh parsley

1 tablespoon balsamic vinegar

1 tablespoon sugar

2 cups (125 g) fresh white bread crumbs

1 cup (60 g) finely grated sharp Cheddar cheese

salt and freshly ground black pepper

1 Heat the oil in the buffet casserole over a medium heat on the stovetop. Add the onion and butternut squash and fry gently until they are lightly colored.

2 Add the eggplant, celery, and zucchini and continue frying, turning the vegetables occasionally, for 4 to 5 minutes. Add the tomatoes with their juice, basil, parsley, vinegar, and sugar with 1 cup (250 ml) of water and plenty of seasoning. Cover and simmer slowly for 1¼ to 1½ hours until the vegetables are tender; the squash will take the longest to soften.

3 When the vegetables are tender, remove the buffet casserole from the heat. Mix together the bread crumbs and cheese with plenty of seasoning and scatter this evenly over the vegetables. Put it immediately under a hot broiler to crisp and brown the top. Serve straight from the buffet casserole.

By halving the ingredients, this recipe can be cooked in the 2½-quart (26 cm) buffet casserole.

A number of other vegetables such as fennel, potatoes, carrots, turnips or bell peppers can be used in this recipe. Do not use vegetables that tend to collapse and lose shape when cooked, such as leeks, because the shape should be retained during cooking.

A little parmesan cheese can also be added to the topping to sharpen the flavor.

WILD MUSHROOM RISOTTO

Serves 4 as an appetizer, or 2 or 3 as a main course

Preparation time: 25 minutes + soaking

Cooking time: 40 minutes

The cost of good dried porcini or chanterelle mushrooms may appear to be high, but only 1 cup (25 g) is required to give this risotto a superb flavor. Unlike the majority of recipes in this book, this one does need attention while it is cooking, but the results are well worth it. Perhaps you can sample the wine and listen to your favorite music while you leisurely stir: very relaxing and therapeutic! A 3½-quart (30 cm) buffet casserole is the ideal shape for this recipe.

1 cup (25 g) loosely packed dried porcini or chanterelle mushrooms
1 tablespoon (15 g) butter, softened
1 tablespoon extra-virgin olive oil
1 medium onion, chopped finely
2 garlic cloves, crushed
1¼ cups (350 g) arborio rice
1¼ cups (125 g) thinly sliced cremini mushrooms
1 cup (250 ml) dry white wine
5 cups (1¼ litres) hot chicken stock

1 teaspoon salt
⅛ teaspoon freshly ground black pepper
1 tablespoon finely grated parmesan cheese, to serve

1 Put the dried mushrooms into a small bowl. Cover with 1 cup (250 ml) very hot water and leave to soak for at least 30 minutes. Drain and reserve the soaking liquid.

2 Melt the butter with the oil in the buffet casserole over medium heat on the stovetop. Add the onion and fry gently until it begins to soften; lower the heat if it begins to color.

3 Add the garlic and rice and stir until all the butter and oil are absorbed. Stir in the cremini mushrooms and roughly chopped soaked mushrooms.

4 Move the buffet casserole away from the heat and stir in 4 tablespoons of the mushroom soaking liquid, taking care not to add the gritty sediment in the bottom. Add the wine and 1 cup (250 ml) of the hot stock

with the seasonings. Return the buffet casserole to the heat, stir well and leave to simmer very gently for 10 to 15 minutes, stirring occasionally.

5 Add another cup (250 ml) of the hot stock and continue simmering and stirring for 10 to 15 minutes longer. Repeat this process another 3 times until all the stock has been used. After the last addition, stir frequently. The consistency should be very moist and creamy with the rice grains soft, but remaining whole. Serve from the buffet casserole with the freshly grated parmesan cheese sprinkled over the top.

 An 11-inch (28 cm) fry pan or sauté pan can also be used for this recipe.

 Fresh wild mushrooms can be found in some supermarkets. Use 1 cup (125 g) of these instead of the dried version.

 The mushrooms in this dish make it well suited to lighter-bodied red wines. A good quality Cru Beaujolais, such as Brouilly or Fleurie or an Italian Barbora are top choices.

CHICKEN ROULADES WITH SPINACH AND CHEESE STUFFING

Serves 6

Preparation time: 30 minutes

Cooking time: approximately 45 minutes

It takes a little more time to prepare this recipe but the cooked result is worth it. A sharp Cheddar cheese is used for the stuffing and sauce, but feta cheese also works well. Don't worry if some of the stuffing cheese escapes into the liquid, because it will all be incorporated into the sauce. The wide shape of the 3½-quart (30 cm) buffet casserole is ideal for this recipe.

6 boned and skinned chicken
    breast halves
¼ teaspoon ground nutmeg
¼ teaspoon dried thyme
4½ ounces (125 g) young spinach
    leaves
8 ounces (225 g) sharp Cheddar
    cheese, in one piece
2 tablespoons vegetable oil
1 small onion, sliced thinly
1 cup (250 ml) hot chicken stock
1 tablespoon cornstarch
1 cup (250 ml) skim milk
salt and freshly ground black
    pepper
boiled plain rice or noodles, to
    serve

1 Place the chicken breast halves between sheets of plastic wrap. Pound them with a heavy rolling pin until they are about twice as large, but not so thin you can see through them.

2 Sprinkle each one with a little nutmeg, thyme, and seasoning, followed by a few leaves of the raw spinach, dividing these equally between the 6 pieces.

3 Cut 6 ounces (175 g) of the cheese into finger-size pieces. Place one in the middle of the spinach on each chicken piece. Roll up the chicken pieces "jelly-roll" fashion, tucking in the side edges to enclose the cheese. Secure with thin string or tooth-picks.

4 Heat the oil in the buffet casserole over medium heat on the stovetop. Add the onion and fry gently until it is just beginning to soften. Add the chicken roulades and brown them evenly on all sides.

5 Gradually add half the hot stock around the roulades with a little seasoning. Cover and simmer slowly for 30 to 40 minutes until the chicken is very tender.

6 Lift the roulades out of the pan and keep them hot on the upturned lid. Carefully remove the strings or toothpicks. Add the remaining stock to the cooking liquid and bring this to a simmer. Blend the cornstarch with a little of the milk, then stir this and the remaining milk into the liquid, simmering and stirring until the sauce thickens. Finely grate the remaining cheese into the sauce, stirring until it melts. Taste and adjust the seasoning before returning the roulades to the sauce to reheat. Serve with boiled plain rice or noodles.

 An 11-inch (28 cm) frypan or sauté pan with a lid can also be used for this recipe.

 Scallops of pork or turkey make a delicious alternative for this dish.

 An off-dry white wine, which has a touch of sweetness, will work well with this combination of ingredients. Try a New World Chenin Blanc or a French Vouvray.

SPICED MEATBALLS WITH LINGUINI

Serves 6
Preparation time: 30 minutes
Cooking time: 40 minutes

The recipe suits the 3-quart (30 cm) buffet casserole very well, because you need a wide, shallow pan to fry the meatballs, then a lid while cooking them. You can, however, also cook this recipe in a large frypan with a lid.

1 pound (450 g) dried linguini

For the meatballs:

1 pound (450 g) ground lean beef
½ pound (225 g) ground lean pork
1 medium onion, chopped finely
2 cups (125 g) fresh white bread
    crumbs
2 teaspoons ground hot chili
    powder
1 teaspoon ground allspice
2 tablespoons fresh chopped
    flat-leaf parsley
½ teaspoon salt
¼ teaspoon freshly ground black
    pepper
1 large egg, beaten
2 tablespoons vegetable oil, for
    frying

For the sauce:

2 tablespoons vegetable oil
1 onion, chopped finely
2 garlic cloves, crushed

1 red bell pepper, seeded,
    quartered, and cut into thin
    slices
1 pound (450 g) canned plum
    tomatoes, chopped, with their
    juice
2 bay leaves
2 tablespoons fresh chopped
    flat-leaf parsley
salt and freshly ground black
    pepper

1 Put all the meatball ingredients into a large bowl and mix thoroughly. Turn out onto a well floured surface and divide into 24 equal pieces.

2 Using wet hands, form each piece into a ball and place them on a cookie baking sheet, spacing them well apart. Cover and refrigerate for at least 1 hour before frying.

3 Heat the oil in the buffet casserole over a medium heat on the stovetop. Add a few meatballs at a time and fry until all are evenly brown; transfer them to the upturned lid as they brown.

4 If necessary add a little more oil to the buffet casserole, then add the onion, garlic, and bell pepper and fry until they begin to soften.

5 Add the tomatoes with their juice, the bay leaves, parsley, and some seasoning.

6 Return the meatballs to the sauce, cover, and simmer for 20 to 30 minutes, turning the meatballs over at least once.

7 While the meatballs are cooking, cook the linguini until it is "al dente"; drain well. Divide the linguini between 6 serving plates and top each with the meatballs and a little sauce.

 If you make the meatballs from fresh ground meat they can be frozen at the end of Step 2, so that they are ready in advance when you want to make the dish. Thaw them before cooking.

 This classic Italian dish deserves a wine of Italian heritage. A good quality Chianti would make an excellent accompaniment or try one of the Sangiovese-based red wines from California.

POACHED SALMON WITH WATERCRESS SAUCE

Serves 4

Preparation time: 15 minutes, including making the sauce

Cooking time: 5 to 8 minutes

This recipe uses the 2½-quart (26 cm) buffet casserole. If you need to cook for six people, use the larger 3½-quart (30 cm) version and increase the quantities by half.

four 6 to 8 ounce (175 to 225 g) thick, boned and skinned salmon fillets
a few fresh parsley sprigs
2 bay leaves
pared zest of 1 lemon
½ cup (125 ml) dry white wine
a little coarse sea salt and freshly ground black pepper

For the watercress sauce:

1 cup (60 g) watercress leaves with fine stems
a small bunch of fresh flat-leaf parsley
1 garlic clove
4 tablespoons mayonnaise
1 teaspoon Dijon mustard
2 teaspoons lemon juice

To serve:

new potatoes
steamed asparagus or zucchini

1 Put the salmon into the buffet casserole with the herbs, lemon zest, wine, and the seasonings. Bring to a slow simmer, cover, and poach for 5 to 8 minutes until the fish flakes easily. Test the fish after 5 minutes so it is not overcooked.

2 While the fish is cooking, make the sauce. Put all the ingredients in a food processor or blender and whizz just long enough to blend the ingredients, but not so as to break down the watercress and herbs completely.

3 Lift out the fish from the buffet casserole and remove any herbs or lemon zest. Serve with a little of the sauce, new potatoes, and steamed asparagus or zucchini.

A large 11-inch (28 cm) covered frypan or sauté pan can also be used for this recipe.

The watercress sauce can be made a day ahead and stored in a covered container in the refrigerator.

The poached salmon can also be served cold with the chilled sauce and a selection of salads.

The top choice for this dish is a dry Champagne or Sparkling wine but a dry white Burgundy from Meursault or Puligny-Montrachet will work equally well. For the more adventurous, a dry Riesling from the Alsace region of France is another option.

POACHED FRUITS IN ORANGE SYRUP

Serves 6

Preparation time: 20 minutes

Cooking time: 35 minutes

This recipe makes full use of the buffet casserole as a cook-and-serve dish. The fruits can be changed to suit personal taste, but do be sure to begin with firm fruits that will hold their shape during poaching. The 2½-quart (26 cm) buffet casserole is used for this recipe.

3 large, firm dessert apples, such as Courtland, Winesap, or York Imperial

3 large, firm dessert pears, such as Bartlett, Bosc or Comice

6 firm apricots

½ cup (125 ml) fresh orange juice

⅓ cup (75 g) sugar

1 cinnamon stick, broken into 2 pieces

finely grated zest of 2 large oranges

⅓ cup (60 g) whole blanched almonds

2 tablespoons Cointreau or any other orange-flavored liqueur

thick plain yogurt or ice cream, to serve

1 Peel, quarter, and core the apples and pears. Halve and remove the pits from the apricots. Set all the fruit aside.

2 Put the orange juice, sugar, and ½ cup (125 ml) water into the buffet casserole. Heat slowly on the stovetop over a low heat to dissolve the sugar, then stir well, adding the cinnamon sticks and orange zest.

3 Put the apple and pear quarters into the syrup, cover, and poach slowly for approximately 20 minutes, depending on the hardness of the fruit. Add the halved apricots and continue poaching for 10 minutes longer.

4 When the fruits are poached, they will be tender but still holding their shape. Uncover and stir in the whole almonds and Cointreau. Remove the buffet from the heat and set aside to let the fruit and syrup cool completely. Cover and chill for 1 to 2 hours before serving with thick plain yogurt or ice cream.

 One-and-a-half times the quantities can be cooked in the 3½-quart (30 cm) version, to serve 9 or 10.

 Without the addition of the Cointreau this makes a delicious breakfast dish which can be eaten with a little yogurt.

 A German Trockenbeerenauslese or Eiswein makes for a rich and wonderful dessert accompaniment. An orange Muscat from California is a less expensive alternative.

SKILLETS, NONSTICK FRYPANS & SAUTÉ PANS

A good skillet or frypan, whether it has a nonstick coating or not, should be very efficient in transmitting heat from the stovetop to the food. Shallow frying is intended to be one of the quicker cooking methods, and if the food is to be crisp yet not greasy on the outside and moist and succulent on the inside, this speed is important.

However, because of the efficiency of cast iron, this speed of cooking does not have to be coupled with high heats. As with all other shapes, the correct frying or searing temperature will be achieved on a medium and then low setting. Satin black porcelain enamel, or the lighter porcelain enamels are not made as, or intended to be, nonstick, but if the rules of medium and low heats are followed an almost nonstick release of food can be achieved. In fact slight sticking of meats such as steaks, chicken or pork on this porcelain enamel surface is a benefit and will result in the correct sealing and searing of the outside, as well as the caramelization of the juices. However, severe sticking of foods on these porcelain enamel surfaces is almost always as a result of the pan being overheated right at the beginning, before the food is even added. Once made very hot, the cast iron is not eager to release its heat and if foods, particularly those such as eggs or omelettes, are added they can stick. If, on the other hand, the pan is placed over a medium heat and allowed to heat through evenly, cooking can begin at speed, but a speed that allows the cook to be in control and not fighting to rescue the frazzled edges of a fried egg while the yolk is still undercooked.

Some shapes in the Le Creuset frypan range have nonstick coatings. A good nonstick pan can be invaluable and if you are not always successful with frying in an uncoated pan, it can make cooking so much easier.

Nonstick coatings do not, however, always enjoy the best reputation for long life. Sadly this is more to do with the way they are used, rather than their quality. Like uncoated cast iron pans they should always be used on medium and low heats. It is a known fact that *no* nonstick coating can withstand continuous high temperature cooking. At high temperatures the surface will soften and at this soft stage will be most vulnerable to damage, either from tools or the heat intensity itself. When repeatedly overheated in this way, the surface will almost always discolor and peel or become thin.

The golden rule with *all* nonstick products (and not just cast iron) is to avoid overheating and, as mentioned earlier when referring to uncoated pans, this also applies to the heat-up time. The heat-retaining qualities of cast iron will allow the temperature in the material to continue to rise for a short while after the heat is lowered and if the heat-up time has been on a high setting the pan will have become very hot indeed, so overheating is inevitable.

However, if a nonstick frypan is used correctly it will, as my own pieces demonstrate, continue to give trouble-free cooking for many years with little or no sign of damage or reduction in the "nonstick" qualities. Even teenagers, who seem to be drawn to nonstick like a magnet, can be educated early on in their culinary lives that not *everything* has to be used at the highest setting possible!

The shape of a good skillet or frypan also has an effect on how it can be used. The low, gently sloped sides of a skillet make for quick cooking and easy turning of foods. The skillet and omelette pans have metal handles, thus extending their use to the broiler or oven. For example a skillet can just as happily be used to make a fruit crumble (see page 46), as it can to cook delicious steaks or fish. Skillets also have pouring lips on each side making the emptying of oil or deglazed sauces so much easier and cleaner. The frypans and sauté pans have more rounded, curved side walls, making the sliding of a spatula under foods extremely easy. The sauté pan also has much deeper sides making the sautéing and tossing of foods easier. A sauté pan allows a greater depth of oil to be used and can accommodate larger pieces of food for frying or pre-browning prior to making a ragoût or casserole. Both the frypans and sauté pans have glass lids available and this obviously extends their usefulness even further because with the lid they can double as a stovetop casserole dish or covered fryer (see the recipe for Sticky Chicken Wings, page 40).

The recipes in this chapter make use of the features both skillets and nonstick frypans offer, not just for frying but for desserts as well. They begin with a reliable step-by-step guide to perfect omelettes – one of the simplest and most satisfying recipes to make well. The range includes three sizes of skillet; an omelette pan; two sizes of nonstick frypan and two sizes of sauté pan.

General Tips

- There is no need to season a porcelain enamelled surface frypan or skillet before use. It can simply be washed, dried and used.
- The nonstick surface does not need seasoning, but a wipe over with an oiled pad of kitchen paper towel before first use will condition the surface.
- Use medium and then low heats for all cooking on all stovetops. Once a pan has reached its frying temperature on a medium setting, that temperature can generally be maintained on a lower setting.
- A little oil, white fat or butter should always be used and when melted should cover the entire surface of the pan. Corn or vegetable oil can be used for most frying. Flavored oils such as olive oil have a lower smoking point, so are best used together with another oil or butter so that over-browning or burning is prevented.
- The oil is hot enough when it takes on a gentle rippled appearance. Butter will bubble and foam but should not be browned before frying begins. If at any time the oil or fat is smoking hot, remove the pan from the heat and allow it to cool before proceeding.
- When searing or sealing meat, poultry or fish, pat the surface dry on paper towels. Wet meat may stick to the surface and introduce water into the oil, thereby cooling it. This may result in a steamed surface on the food, rather than a browned appearance. Marinated foods should also be patted dry before frying.
- Nonstick surfaces can, with care, be used with no extra oil at all, but do remember that even the smallest amount will improve the fried appearance and flavor of the food.
- Do not leave an empty nonstick pan heating unattended. This is one of the quickest ways to damage it.

- To prolong the life of nonstick surfaces you should use heat-resistant silicone, nylon or wooden tools. Metal blades and tools can be used with extreme care, but can cause scratching of the surface.
- Satin black porcelain enamel skillets will take on a "patina" once in use for some time. This will make the surface appear slightly discolored and black, but this is normal and aids the release of foods – particularly eggs and pancakes. It is therefore unwise to attempt to clean this off or dishwash these pieces as both procedures will reduce the patina and the ease with which foods lift off the surface.
- All pans will be very hot once frying has been completed. Always cool the piece for several minutes before filling with warm water for soaking or washing. Never plunge a hot pan into cold water, or fill with cold water.

Each piece is accompanied by its own detailed care and use booklet. Always refer to this before you begin using a new pan, particularly the warranty details for the nonstick coatings.

CLASSIC OMELETTE WITH PARMESAN CHEESE AND CHIVES

Serves 1

Preparation time: 2 to 3 minutes

Cooking time: 3 minutes

There is much controversy about what makes a perfect omelette and how it should be cooked – and all this for one of the world's simplest dishes to make! The real key to success is very fresh eggs, preferably at room temperature, unsalted butter (you cannot cut down on the butter because it's simply part of the recipe), and a good heavy omelette pan or skillet at the correct temperature. This recipe serves one person and should be cooked in the 8-inch (20 cm) omelette pan. A nonstick surface obviously makes the task a little easier and reliable, but if a black porcelain enameled pan is correctly heated the omelette will not stick.

2 large eggs
1 tablespoon (15 g) unsalted butter
1 tablespoon freshly grated
    parmesan cheese
1 teaspoon freshly snipped chives
a little salt and freshly ground black
    pepper

1 Beat the eggs and seasonings lightly together in a small bowl until the yolks and whites are just broken into each other. Melt the butter in the pan over medium heat. As the butter melts, tilt the pan so it completely covers the bottom. When the butter almost ceases to foam and is just on the point of coloring, pour in the eggs. Do not begin heating the pan on a high setting, thinking it will save time, because it won't. If the pan is overheated it will take time to cool to the correct temperature and the omelette will be overcolored and tough on the outside, while undercooked on the inside. Overheating may also cause the omelette to stick to a satin black enamel surface.

2 As soon as the eggs are in the pan, use the back of a fork in a circular movement to gently move the eggs from the sides to the

middle of the pan. Tilt the pan so the runny egg at the middle flows to the side. Continue to cook for about 30 seconds until the eggs are just set, but still creamy on the top. Turn off the heat because there will be sufficient retained heat to complete cooking.

3 Scatter the cheese and chives over the surface and immediately slide a spatula under the side of the omelette nearest to the handle. Tipping the pan away from you, roll the omelette out of the pan onto a warmed serving plate. Serve immediately so the omelette remains soft and creamy inside.

 A 9-inch (23 cm) skillet or nonstick frypan can also be used for this recipe.

 Some people (such as the elderly, infants, pregnant women and anyone who is ill) can be allergic to raw or undercooked egg. If this is the case, either cook for a minute *or so longer or slide the pan under a hot broiler for a few seconds to cook the top surface before rolling out of the pan.*

STICKY CHICKEN WINGS

Serves 4
Preparation time: 15 minutes
Cooking time: 25 minutes

These wings are finished with a spicy, sticky sauce. The combination of frying and steaming makes the chicken meat very moist and tender, but to achieve this you need to use a frypan or sauté pan with a lid. Because the sauce is so sticky, a nonstick surface on the pan makes the clean up much easier. Use an 11-inch (28 cm) frypan and lid for this recipe.

2 teaspoons corn oil
2 teaspoons sesame oil
2 shallots, chopped finely
1 garlic clove, crushed
½-inch (1 cm) piece fresh ginger, peeled and chopped
2 pounds 4 ounces (1 kg) chicken wings

For the sauce:
2 tablespoons soy sauce
1 tablespoon Worcestershire sauce
4 tablespoons tomato ketchup
2 tablespoons honey
2 tablespoons orange juice
1 teaspoon cornstarch
salt and freshly ground black pepper

1 Heat both oils together in the pan over a medium heat. Add the shallots, garlic, and ginger, and fry for 2 to 3 minutes to release the flavors. Move to one side of the pan.

2 Add the chicken wings and brown them evenly; season well. Cover the pan and continue cooking over low heat for 10 to 15 minutes or until the chicken is tender and cooked through.

3 Meanwhile, mix all the sauce ingredients together.

4 Remove the lid and, if necessary, drain off any excess oil from the pan. Pour in the sauce and cook over medium heat, stirring occasionally, until it thickens and coats the chicken: it should be thick and sticky. Taste and season the sauce before serving.

 A 2½-quart (26 cm) buffet casserole can also be used for this recipe.

 These chicken wings are just as tasty served cold with salads.

WHOLEWHEAT BLINIS

SKILLETS, NONSTICK FRYPANS & SAUTÉ PANS

**Makes about 75 x 2-inch
(5 cm) blinis**

**Preparation time: 10 minutes
for the batter + standing;
15 minutes for the toppings**

Cooking time: 30 minutes

*These are extremely easy to make
and are versatile buffet or appetizer
bases. They can be made hours,
or even weeks, in advance of a
party because they freeze well (see
Cook's Tip). These are best made
in an 11-inch (28 cm) nonstick
frypan. If the cooking surface is
satin black porcelain enamel and
not nonstick, make sure you re-oil
the surface between batches.*

For the blinis:
1 cup (125 g) wholewheat flour
1 cup (125 g) all-purpose flour
1 envelope of active-dry yeast
1 teaspoon salt
1½ cups (375 ml) warmed milk
2 large eggs
vegetable oil, for frying

For the toppings:
1 cup (225 g) herb-flavored or
    plain cream cheese
2 tablespoons heavy cream
2 cups (125 g) cooked small,
    shelled shrimp

4½ ounces (125 g) smoked
    salmon, cut into narrow strips
a little caviar or black lumpfish roe
salt and freshly ground black
    pepper
some chives and parsley, to
    garnish

1 To make the blinis, put both
the flours into a large bowl with the
yeast and salt. Stir in the warmed
milk with the beaten eggs. Cover
loosely with plastic wrap and leave
to stand in a warm place for 1 to
1½ hours until the mixture is almost
double in volume.

2 Heat the pan over medium
heat and brush with a little oil. Drop
5 or 6 spoonfuls of the batter,
spaced apart, into the pan and
cook until the blinis are golden
brown underneath and bubbling on
top. Turn them over and cook the
other side; remove from the pan
and leave to cool.

3 Lightly oil the pan between
batches (with a nonstick pan you
need very little oil) and continue
cooking blinis until all the batter is
used.

4 To make the toppings, beat
together the cream cheese and
cream with a little seasoning until
the consistency is soft enough for
easy spreading or piping.

5 Spread or pipe a small
amount of the cream cheese
topping on the top of each blini.
Alternate between adding 1 or 2
shrimp, or twisted smoked salmon
strips to each. Garnish with the roe
and a few chives or parsley. When
serving, the blinis look most
dramatic if put into rows of all the
same topping.

*A skillet or flat-surface grill
can also be used for this
recipe.*

*To freeze the plain blinis, leave
them to cool completely and
place them in plastic boxes,
interleaved with waxed paper.
Freeze for up to 2 months.*

*Thaw before finishing with the topping.
For a vegetarian alternative, place
small pieces of roasted vegetables on
top of the cream cheese.*

PEPPERED STEAKS WITH WINE SAUCE

Serves 4

Preparation time: 15 minutes

Cooking time: 10 minutes for the sauce, 4 to 6 minutes for the steaks

If you have access to two skillets, or one frypan and a skillet, cook the steaks and sauce side by side. If not, make the sauce first, keep it hot in another pan and then add to the steaks at the end. Use an 11-inch (28 cm) frypan or iron-handle skillet.

four 8 ounce (225 g) good-quality
   steaks, such as filet, sirloin, or
   small porterhouse
2 tablespoons vegetable oil
2 tablespoons black peppercorns,
   crushed
½ teaspoon coarse sea salt

For the wine sauce:

1 tablespoon (15 g) butter,
   softened
1 tablespoon vegetable oil
2 shallots, chopped finely
1 garlic clove, crushed
1 tablespoon all-purpose flour
1 cup (250 ml) port wine or other
   sweet red wine
1 teaspoon mild prepared mustard
1 teaspoon sugar
1 tablespoon tomato paste

1 Prepare the steaks by brushing both sides with a little of the oil, then turn them in a mixture of the peppercorns and salt, pressing it well into the surface.

2 To make the sauce, melt the butter with the oil in the frypan or skillet over medium heat. Add the shallots and fry, stirring, until they begin to soften. Add the garlic and fry for 1 minute longer.

3 Add the flour and stir until it absorbs the excess butter and oil. Gradually stir in the port, mustard, sugar, and tomato paste with seasoning to taste. Simmer slowly, while cooking the steaks.

4 To cook the steaks, heat the remaining vegetable oil in another pan over medium heat. When hot, add the steaks and cook for 2 to 3 minutes on each side, adjusting the cooking time to suit personal taste. Take care when cooking because the peppercorns will give off a pungent aroma; use an overhead extractor if possible. When the steaks are cooked, pour the sauce into the pan, warm

through briefly and serve with a little of the sauce spooned around the steaks.

 This recipe can also be cooked in the base of a 3½-quart (30 cm) buffet casserole.

 Thick, sliced lamb from the leg can be used instead of steak.

 A full-bodied red wine is the perfect partner for the steak. A Cabernet Sauvignon or Syrah from California or Australia are top choices. A peppery, bold California Zinfandel will also work well. You may want to use the same wine for the sauce.

MEDITERRANEAN CRISP COD

Serves 6

Preparation time: 20 minutes + standing and chilling times for the fish

Cooking time: 10 minutes

Freshly caught cod, pan-fried with a light coating of crumbs, is hard to beat for flavor and with this Mediterranean-style crumb topping, the fish remains flaky and moist. Sprinkling the fish with a little salt 1 hour before cooking makes the flesh "plump up" and hold together better during frying. Use an 11-inch (28 cm) nonstick frypan, or iron-handle skillet for this recipe.

2 teaspoons coarse sea salt
six 6 ounce (175 g) cod steaks, filleted and skinned
2 cups (125 g) fresh white bread crumbs
finely grated zest of 1 large lemon
1 teaspoon dried marjoram
1 teaspoon dried parsley
8 pitted black olives, chopped finely
¼ teaspoon salt
a pinch of freshly ground black pepper
3 tablespoons all-purpose flour
2 large eggs, well beaten
4 tablespoons vegetable oil, for frying
lemon wedges, to serve

1. Scatter the salt over the fish, cover, and leave in the refrigerator for 1 hour. Rinse the fish in cold water and pat dry with paper towels.

2. Mix together the bread crumbs, lemon zest, herbs, olives, and the seasonings; transfer to a large plate.

3. Working with one fish steak at a time, dip the fish first in the flour and then the beaten egg before coating it with the crumb mixture, pressing the crumbs on to the surface. Chill again for 30 minutes to 1 hour, if possible.

4. Heat the oil in the pan over medium heat until there is a very light ripple in the oil surface. Add the cod pieces and fry for 4 to 5 minutes on each side until the coating is crisp and golden brown. You might need to lower the heat a little when the fish is turned to prevent over-browning.

5. Serve immediately with the lemon wedges.

 This recipe can also be cooked in the base of a 3½-quart (30 cm) buffet casserole.

 Other firm fish such as halibut, swordfish, or monkfish can also be used for this recipe.

 A crisp, light-bodied, dry white wine will work best with the cod. A New World Sauvignon Blanc from the United States or New Zealand will be an excellent pairing. A crisp Chablis from Burgundy or a Sparkling wine would also work well.

APRICOT SPICED CRÊPES

Makes twelve 8-inch (20 cm) crêpes (serves 4)

Preparation time: 10 minutes for the batter, 5 minutes for the filling

Cooking time: 20 minutes

Crêpes are very special, paper-thin buttery "pancakes", and are very French. They have a host of uses, both sweet and savory, and can be both large and small, so they can feature in almost any meal at any time of the day. Crêpes freeze well, so they can be made in advance (see Cook's Tips, below). Use a 23 cm skillet or 24 cm frypan.

For the crêpe batter:

1 cup (125 g) all-purpose flour

¼ teaspoon salt

2 large eggs

1 cup (250 ml) milk

2 tablespoons (30 g) unsalted
   butter, melted and cooled

vegetable oil, for frying

For the filling:

1 pound (450 g) canned apricot
   halves, drained

3 tablespoons crème fraîche or
   sour cream

½ teaspoon apple pie spice

To serve:

a little sugar

ice cream, crème fraîche or sour
   cream

1 To make the batter, sift the flour and salt into a bowl. Make a well in the middle, add the eggs and half the milk. Whisk until smooth.

2 Whisk in the remaining milk and cooled butter. Leave the batter to stand for 1 to 2 hours before using. If the consistency thickens after standing, add 2 to 3 tablespoons of milk: it should be similar to unwhipped whipping cream.

3 While the crêpe batter is standing, make the filling. Put the drained apricots into a blender or food processor with the crème fraîche or sour cream and apple pie spice; blend until smooth.

4 To cook the crêpes, heat the pan over medium heat, wiping the surface with a little oil. When hot, add about ¼ cup (60 ml) of batter, swirling it around the pan to completely cover the bottom. Cook until bubbles begin to rise through the surface. Turn the crêpe over and cook the other side until it is pale golden brown.

5 Slide the crêpe out of the pan and stack on a plate; they will not stick together, so pile them on top of one another. Cover with a piece of aluminum foil to keep warm.

6 When all the crêpes are cooked, spread about 2 teaspoons of the apricot purée over one half of each and roll up or fold into quarters.

7 Sprinkle with a little sugar and serve warm with ice cream, crème fraîche, or sour cream.

 Smaller crêpes can be made in the omelette pan.

 The crêpe batter can also be made in a blender or food processor. This does make the batter a little foamy, however, so leave it for the full standing time until the foam subsides.

Skim or 2% milk will make lighter crêpes, but whole milk makes a slightly firmer consistency that can be easier to handle during cooking.

Cooked crêpes can be frozen for 2 to 3 months. Wrap them in batches of 4–6 so that you can remove the quantity you need from the freezer.

RHUBARB AND ORANGE CRUMBLE

Serves 6

Preparation time: 20 minutes

Cooking time: 20 to 25 minutes

An iron-handle skillet is not just useful for savory dishes or steaks cooked on the stovetop. It also makes an ideal baking pan for fruit crumbles, cobblers, or cakes. This dessert is simple to make and can be eaten hot or cold with ice cream, whipped cream, or thick plain yogurt. Use a 10-inch (26 cm) iron-handle skillet for this recipe.

1 pound 10 ounces (750 g) young rhubarb
heaping ½ cup (125 g) sugar
finely grated zest of 1 orange
¼ cup (60 ml) orange juice
butter, for the skillet

For the crumble:
2 cups (250 g) sifted all-purpose flour
1 stick (125 g) chilled butter, diced
¼ cup (60 g) white sugar
½ cup (60 g) slivered almonds

1 Preheat the oven to 350°F/180°C/Gas Mark 4. Cut the rhubarb into ½-inch (1 cm) pieces and put them into the lightly-buttered skillet.

2 Stir in the sugar, orange zest and juice.

3 To make the crumble topping, put the flour, butter, sugar, and half the almonds into a food processor and process until the mixture resembles fine bread crumbs. If you do not have a food processor, cut or rub the butter into the flour, then add the sugar and half the almonds, crushed.

4 Spoon the crumble over the top of the rhubarb, pressing it down lightly. Scatter the remaining almonds evenly over the top.

5 Bake in the middle of the oven for 20 to 25 minutes, until the top is firm and pale golden brown. Serve straight from the skillet.

The base of a 2½-quart (26 cm) buffet casserole can also be used for this recipe.

If you or your guests have a nut allergy, omit the almonds.
This recipe is also delicious using fresh pitted and halved apricots.

APPLE TARTE TATIN

Serves 6 to 8
Preparation time: 15 minutes
Cooking time: 30 minutes

Tarte Tatin is French through and through. The "recipe" was accidentally achieved by a mishap in the kitchens of the Hotel Tatin in the town of Lamotte-Beuvron, deep in the Loire Valley.

The Tatin sisters, Caroline and Stephanie, had inherited the hotel from their father in 1888. Caroline was the business manager, while Stephanie was the cook. Stephanie's cooking had a good reputation, her apple tart was renowned. One day, however, she lightly cooked the apples and butter as usual, but then, in haste, or by mistake, put the pastry crust over the top of them, instead of putting the apples into a pastry shell. She may have realised her mistake, but too late, it was done, and so the tart was baked. To serve this dessert Stephanie needed to make it appear to be her usual apple tart, so she turned it upside down. Her diners loved it. In the oven, the apples, sugar, and butter had intensified their caramel flavor and the pastry crust was dry, light, and crisp.

Unknown to Stephanie, her mistake was to become a piece of culinary history and has enjoyed growing popularity worldwide ever since.

A 10-inch (26 cm) iron-handle skillet is a good choice for this recipe.

⅓ cup (75 g) white sugar
⅓ cup (75 g) butter
5 large dessert apples, such as Golden Delicious
2 tablespoons lemon juice
8 ounces (225 g) store-bought puff pastry dough
whipped cream or ice cream, to serve

1 Peel, quarter, and core the apples; cover with cold water to prevent discoloration.

2 Preheat the oven to 400°F/200°C/Gas Mark 6. Put the sugar and butter in the skillet or Tatin dish and melt the butter over medium heat on the stovetop, stirring to dissolve the sugar evenly.

3 Drain the apples well, then place them rounded side down to tightly fill the pan's bottom; sprinkle with the lemon juice. Cook over the same heat for approximately 5 minutes until the sugar and butter begin to caramelize, but not color too much at this stage.

4 Remove the skillet from the heat and leave to cool for a few minutes while rolling out the dough. Roll the dough into a circle the same size as the top of the dish. Place it lightly over the apples, tucking the edges down around the fruit so it forms a rim to contain the filling when it is turned out. Make four small steam holes.

5 Transfer to the oven and bake on the top shelf for 15 to 20 minutes until the dough is well risen and golden brown.

6 Leave the tart to rest for 5 minutes before loosening around the edge with a round-bladed knife. Invert onto a wide, shallow plate with a rim to catch any caramel. Serve warm with whipped cream or ice cream.

 Hot off the line is a custom-made Le Creuset Tatin dish with cleverly designed handles for easy "turn over" which is ideal for this recipe.

 Plums, peaches, nectarines, or apricots can be used instead of apples. Cut each in half and remove the pits.

Calvados, applejack, or cognac can be used instead of lemon juice.

 A sweet Muscat makes an excellent partner for this traditional French dessert. Look for a Muscat Beaumes-de-Venise or a California version of the wine.

GRILLS & SKILLET GRILLS

The desire to spend time in the kitchen cooking for ourselves or the family sometimes loses its appeal. I love cooking, but there are times when you look for the easy option, open the freezer door and see what ready meals there are, or phone for a take-out, or go out to a local restaurant. But there is a better solution and it is perhaps the quickest, the most relaxing and the healthiest of them all. All you need to do is take a steak or a piece of fish out of the freezer and leave it to thaw while you shower and relax. Then, with the aid of a ribbed grill or skillet grill, take just a few minutes to cook something really tasty and satisfying.

In recent years, there has been an explosion of interest in grills, particularly ribbed grills. They have the appeal of being able to instantly recreate that delicious seared flavor with a piece of steak or a piece of fish that can only normally be enjoyed when you go out to a "grill" restaurant. While the notion that we should eat healthier and more nutritious meals at all times is not always what we want to be reminded of at the end of a tiring day, the health benefits of cooking on a grill are very easily obtained.

The most significant health benefit when cooking with a ribbed grill is the reduction of the amount of fat which the food will have when you eat it. As the food cooks, any draining fat will collect below the ribs and be contained there. The food never sits in oil or fat so it cannot re-absorb it while it cooks. The ribs themselves are carefully designed to be wide enough to support the food and give the desired seared pattern, but are narrow enough to prevent sticking. Very little oil is required for greasing the ribs and, as the grill ages, almost no extra oil is needed at all.

Other healthy benefits include the retention of vitamins and minerals; the outside of the food seals quickly so there is less likelihood of these leaching out and the speed of cooking retains the maximum amount of moisture and flavor.

When you want to introduce other flavors you can, when time is short, baste the food with your favorite dressing. But if you have a little more time, marinating, even with the simplest of ingredients, will enhance the flavors and tenderize tougher fibres. Vegetables such as bell peppers, zucchini, eggplant, tomatoes and mushrooms also respond well to grilling. They can become a meal in themselves and are absolutely delicious when cold in salads.

But the grill itself, and the material it is made from, are all important for successful cooking. Cast iron has long been the preferred material for grilling not least because it has the strength to withstand the high temperatures a grill will achieve. Nonstick surfaces on grills are not successful because they simply cannot withstand these temperatures. A satin black porcelain enamel finish, on the other hand, gives almost the same nonstick benefit but without the inevitable destruction of the surface. The porcelain enamel surface is also ready to use when you take the grill home; no seasoning is required and little or no additional oiling between uses.

The Le Creuset range of grills includes flat ribbed grills, reversible grills, with one side flat for pancakes and the reverse side ribbed, and skillet grills with deeper sides. All have metal handles so they can be used on the stovetop, under the broiler or in the oven. This chapter includes recipes showing how all of these methods can be used, but the step-by-step Cilantro

Limed Chicken with Chili-Lime Mayonnaise on page 51 takes you through the basic foolproof method you should adopt for all foods. These steps will ensure perfect results.

General Tips

- Le Creuset grills are designed for stovetop, broiler and oven use and, as a result, have metal handles. These handles, even on the stovetop, will get hot quite quickly, so before you begin cooking make sure an oven mitt, cloth or handle glove is available.
- The most important tip, or perhaps rule, when using a cast iron grill is not to overheat it. It does not need to be preheated on a high heat or indeed used on a high heat at all to achieve good grilled results. In fact, if you do adopt this method, the food and the grill will suffer and cleaning become more difficult. Remember, cast iron is excellent at retaining heat and, once overheated and smoking, the outside of the food will be charred (which is not as healthy) long before the centre is cooked.
- A grill, flat or ribbed and whatever size or shape, should *always* be preheated on a medium heat setting allowing the heat to be absorbed and spread evenly throughout the piece. Surprisingly, this doesn't take a long time and once the surface is hot the searing and pattern of sear lines you want to achieve will result automatically, and the grilled result will be delicious and moist all the way through.
- Grilling foods that are dry or almost dry on the outside will give best results. The sear lines will not be as pronounced if the food is wet and wet food often sticks to the surface because it lowers the surface temperatures. Even a steak or a chop purchased from the local supermarket should have the surface dried by patting it between sheets of paper towel. If a recipe uses a marinade, the excess should also be patted off before grilling begins.
- The amount of oil required to oil the ribs or surface will very much depend on the age of the grill. The frequency of use and age will determine how much of a "surface" the grill has produced. This "surface" is called a "patina" and is essential if you want to achieve a surface that will eventually not need any extra fat or oil at all. Therefore the patina, which imparts a brownish-black coloring to the surface, should not be scrubbed off and should not be dishwashed, as this too will reduce its efficiency.
- The best oils to use for greasing the grill are one of the many vegetable or corn oils, lightly applied with a brush, pad or paper towel or sprayed on from an oil sprayer. Olive oil is extremely healthy and has many uses and benefits but the oiling of hot grills with olive oil will result in undesirable smoking. Instead use olive oil to brush over the food or for marinating it.
- With a little experience it is not difficult to judge when a grill is hot enough for grilling to begin. (If it is ever smoking it is too hot and should be cooled.) There is, however, a simple test you can use. Heat the grill with no oil for 2 to 3 minutes on a medium setting. Take a few drops of water on your fingers and drop these over the center of the surface. If they sizzle and evaporate almost immediately, it is hot and ready for use. If the water produces steam and has no sizzle, heat a little longer and repeat the test again. When it is hot enough, oil lightly.
- If you are trying to achieve clearly defined sear lines, do not move the food over the grill surface. Place the food and leave it undisturbed for a few minutes. When the edge of the food is lifted and it comes away easily from the surface, it is ready to turn over. Usually the sear lines at this stage are distinct and beautifully caramelized.

- If you want to produce the rather attractive two-way pattern of lines, (or diamond shapes), on the food surface, it will be necessary to make the first set of lines as described in the point above. Then move the food around a quarter turn, so that the rib lines can lay a mark across the food in the opposite direction.
- The oil or fat collected between the ribs should be discarded, particularly if you wish to make an "au jus" sauce on the grill. The grill should be cooled slightly before cold liquid or wine is added and then returned to the heat to bubble and lift the grilling residues away from the surface. If there are a lot of "bits" in the "jus", you may want to strain it as it is poured out of the grill.
- Cleaning a grill is not, and does not have to be, difficult. The secret is to cool the grill a little, but not let it go completely cold (otherwise residues may stick more firmly to the surface). Then fill, or soak with warm water for 10 to 15 minutes; this can usually be done while you eat. Once the soaking water is discarded, a stiff nylon brush can be used to brush between the ribs before washing and rinsing thoroughly. If residues do become really stuck on, soak for longer in warm water. If the grill has deeper sides, boil some water in it before washing. As the surface browns and discolors, try to accept that this is best for the surface and will ultimately lead to oil- and fat-free cooking altogether.

CILANTRO LIMED CHICKEN WITH CHILI-LIME MAYONNAISE

Serves 6

Preparation time: 15 minutes + marinating

Cooking time: 10 minutes

This is one of the simplest recipes for a Le Creuset grill. Once the chicken is cooked, it can be served hot with vegetables or salads, or left to cool then sliced and mixed with salad ingredients. This recipe uses the 10-inch (26 cm) square skillet grill, but any ribbed grill can be used.

6 chicken breast halves, boned and skinned
2 tablespoons corn oil
finely grated zest of 2 limes
4 tablespoons lime juice
2 tablespoons fresh chopped cilantro
extra corn oil, for brushing
a little freshly ground black pepper

For the chili-lime mayonnaise:

4 tablespoons low-fat mayonnaise
1 small red chili, seeded and chopped finely
finely grated zest of 1 lime
2 teaspoons lime juice
a little salt and freshly ground black pepper

1 Put the chicken pieces into a large Le Creuset gratin dish. Add the oil, lime zest and juice, cilantro, and pepper and turn the chicken so it is coated evenly in the marinade. Cover and leave to stand for a minimum of 1 hour in the refrigerator. Before cooking, lift the chicken out of the marinade and pat dry with paper towels. Meanwhile, mix all the mayonnaise ingredients together, cover, and chill until ready to serve.

2 Heat the ungreased grill over medium heat on the stovetop for 2 to 3 minutes. Test the surface temperature by sprinkling a little cold water over the middle: if the water "spits" and evaporates almost immediately the grill's surface is hot enough to begin cooking. If, however, the water softly sizzles and does not quickly evaporate the surface is not hot enough, so continue heating and retest after 30 seconds to 1 minute.

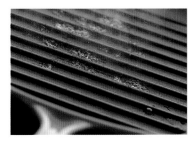

3 Oil the ribs lightly. Place the chicken pieces side by side on the grill and do not move them until you are ready to turn them over, otherwise the distinctive sear lines will not be produced. Grill for 3 to 4 minutes.

4 Lift one edge of a piece of chicken and if it releases easily from the surface it is ready to turn over. If it feels a little tight to lift, leave it for about a minute longer, then turn over. Cook on the other side for 3 to 4 minutes.

5 Serve with a few sprigs of fresh cilantro and a little of the chili-lime mayonnaise on the side.

This method and recipe can also be used for boneless turkey and pork.

The mayonnaise can be stored in a sealed container in the refrigerator for 4 to 5 days.

To check that the chicken is cooked through, pierce the thickest part with a fine blade or toothpick. If the juices run clear, it is cooked. If the juices are pink, continue cooking for a little longer.

GRILLED MEDITERRANEAN VEGETABLES WITH DIPPING SAUCE

Serves 4 to 6
Preparation time: 10 minutes
Cooking time: 20 minutes

This recipe makes a flavorsome hot appetizer, or side vegetable dish to serve with broiled or barbecued steaks, chicken, or fish. Any ribbed grill or skillet grill can be used for this recipe.

two 12 ounce (350g) firm
    eggplants
4 medium zucchini
extra corn oil, for brushing
extra olive oil, for drizzling

For the marinade:

5 tablespoons olive oil
5 tablespoons corn oil
2 teaspoons Italian seasoning
½ teaspoon cayenne pepper
1 teaspoon coarse sea salt

For the dipping sauce:

1 cup (250 g) thick plain yogurt
1 garlic clove, crushed
2 teaspoons fresh chopped
    flat-leaf parsley
finely grated zest of 1 lemon

1 Remove the ends from the eggplants and zucchini. Cut each vegetable into horizontal slices, ½-inch (1 cm) thick. Transfer to a large Le Creuset gratin dish. Mix all the marinade ingredients together and pour over the vegetables, turning them with your hands to make sure they are evenly coated; leave to stand for 1 hour.

2 Meanwhile, mix all the ingredients for the dipping sauce together and leave to stand for 1 hour.

3 Drain the vegetables and pat off any excess marinade with paper towels.

4 Heat the grill over medium heat on the stovetop and brush the ribs lightly with corn oil when it is hot. Add the vegetables, a few at a time, and grill for 2 to 3 minutes on each side. Transfer to a warm serving dish and keep hot while cooking the remaining vegetables.

5 Just before serving, drizzle a little olive oil over. Serve with the dipping sauce.

If left to cool completely, these vegetables can also be used in salads. They are especially good mixed with diced mozzarella cheese, cherry tomatoes, and green olives with a generous drizzle of olive oil over the top.

JERK PORK AND PINEAPPLE KEBABS

Serves 4
Preparation time: 20 minutes
Cooking time: 15 minutes

This recipe is hot, spicy, and slightly sweet. The pineapple juice acts as a tenderizer on the pork so do use fresh pineapple when you can, but canned chunks are a good substitute. Using a giant meat grill for this recipe means all the kebabs can be cooked at once, but any of the smaller grills are ideal too, if you cook the kebabs in two batches.

2 pounds 4 ounces (1 kg) pork
    tenderloin
1 medium fresh pineapple

For the jerk marinade:
4 tablespoons pineapple juice
2 tablespoons corn oil
1 tablespoon malt vinegar
2 small red chilies, seeded and
    chopped finely
2 tablespoons fresh chopped
    cilantro
1 tablespoon fresh chopped thyme
½ teaspoon ground allspice
2 teaspoons sugar

To serve:
rice or baked sweet potatoes
salads

1 You need eight 9-inch (23 cm) wooden or metal kebab skewers. If using wooden skewers, soak them in warm water for 10 minutes, so they will not scorch during cooking.

2 Trim any fat or sinews from the tenderloin and cut as evenly as possible into 1-inch (2.5 cm) chunks.

3 Peel the pineapple and cut it into 1-inch (2.5 cm) thick slices. Cut the slices into 1-inch (2.5 cm) chunks; save as much of the juice as you can while cutting the pineapple, squeezing the outer peel as well.

4 Thread the pork and pineapple evenly onto the skewers then place in a large, shallow dish, such as a Le Creuset gratin dish.

5 Mix together all the ingredients for the marinade, reserving 1 tablespoon of the cilantro for garnish, and pour evenly over the kebabs. Cover and chill for 1 hour, then turn the kebabs in the marinade and chill them for 1 hour longer.

6 Heat the grill over a medium heat on the stovetop and brush lightly with oil when it is hot. Pat the kebabs dry. Grill the kebabs for 3 to 4 minutes on each side, turning them around at least 3 times to make sure the pork is evenly cooked. Sprinkle with the cilantro before serving with rice or baked sweet potatoes and salads.

 Diced chicken or firm fish, such as monkfish, can also be used in this recipe. If using fish, grill for only 1 to 2 minutes on each side.

 The combination of hot spice and sweetness in this dish makes it perfect for a Gewurztraminer: try one from the Anderson Valley in California or from Germany. Riesling or Pinot Gris from Alsace are also excellent candidates.

SPICED DUCK WITH GARLIC POTATO CAKES AND MANGO SALSA

Serves 4

Preparation time: 20 minutes + plus marinating and chilling

Cooking time: 20 minutes for the potatoes, 15 to 20 minutes for the duck

This recipe illustrates perfectly the flexible use of a skillet grill on the stovetop and then in the oven.

4 boned duck breast fillets (skin removed for lower-fat meal)

For the marinade:

3 tablespoons dark soy sauce
3 tablespoons red wine
1 tablespoon light brown sugar
finely grated zest of 1 orange
2 tablespoons orange juice
1-inch (2.5 cm) piece of fresh ginger, peeled and grated
1 teaspoon apple pie spice

For the potato cakes:

1 pound 10 ounces (750 g) potatoes, peeled
1 teaspoon salt
3 large garlic cloves, quartered
4 to 5 tablespoons milk
1 tablespoon (15 g) butter
a little freshly ground black pepper

For the mango salsa:

1 tablespoon corn oil
3 scallions, chopped

1 large, firm mango, peeled and cut into ½-inch (1 cm) dice
½ cup (60 g) raisins
2 tablespoons lemon juice
1 tablespoon light brown sugar
salt and freshly ground black pepper

1 Make several deep slashes through the skin of the duck. Lay in a single layer in a large gratin dish.

2 Mix together all the marinade ingredients and pour over the duck. Cover and chill for 1 hour, then turn the duck over and continue marinating for 1 hour longer.

3 Cook the potatoes in boiling, salted water with the garlic. Drain well and mash thoroughly with the milk, butter, and a little more seasoning. When cool enough to handle, and using wet hands, divide into 8 equal portions. Shape each portion into a round patty about ½-inch (1 cm) thick. Transfer to a greased cookie sheet and brush with a little milk. Cover and chill for at least 30 minutes.

4 To make the salsa, heat the oil in a saucepan over medium

heat. Add the scallions and fry until they are soft, but not brown. Add all the remaining ingredients; lower the heat and simmer, stirring occasionally, for about 10 minutes until the mango begins to soften. Taste and adjust the seasoning accordingly; it should be slightly sweet and sour. Preheat the oven to 400°F/200°C/Gas Mark 6.

5 Heat the grill over a medium heat on the stovetop and brush lightly with oil when it is hot. Drain the duck breasts and pat off any excess marinade with paper towels. Grill the breasts, skin side down, for 2 minutes, then turn over and grill for 2 minutes longer. Carefully pour off any excess fat from the grill.

6 Transfer the grill to the middle of the oven, with the cookie sheet of potato cakes on the rack above. Cook for 10 to 15 minutes. 10 minutes should produce duck that is slightly pink; 15 minutes and it will be well done. Serve the duck immediately with the potato cakes and the mango salsa on the side.

 An iron-handle skillet or buffet casserole base can also be used for this recipe.

 Chicken breasts also work well here. Cook through thoroughly in the oven; they must not be pink inside.

GRILLED STEAK WITH MELTED CHEESE

Serves 4
Preparation time: 5 minutes
Cooking time: about 25 minutes

Use this recipe for any good-quality steak, grilled as your family prefers it. The cheese topping suggested here is a blue cheese, but your favorite cheese can also be used. This recipe can be cooked on any ribbed grill or skillet grill that fits under your broiler.

a little corn oil, for greasing
4 fillet or sirloin steaks, each
    1-inch (2.5 cm) thick
8 ounces (225 g) blue cheese,
    such as roquefort, dolcelatte, or
    gorgonzola
a little coarse sea salt and freshly
    ground black pepper

1 Heat the grill over medium heat on the stovetop. Lightly grease the surface of the grill when it is hot.

2 Dry the surface of the steaks with paper towels, then season well.

3 Grill the steaks for 2½ to 3 minutes on each side for rare steaks; 4 to 5 minutes on each side for medium; 5 to 6 minutes on each side for well done. Meanwhile, heat the broiler on high.

4 As soon as the steaks are cooked, crumble the blue cheese over the top and immediately transfer the grill to the broiler. Broil just until the cheese begins to melt; it will continue melting as it is served.

5 Take the sizzle to the table by serving the steaks straight from the grill. Place a thick, heatproof mat under the grill because it will be very hot.

 Although it won't produce sear lines, a flat surface skillet could also be used for this recipe.

 Salt draws the blood from meat making the fibers tough, so add the salt just before cooking commences.

 A sweet and fruity red such as a Shiraz/Syrah or a soft open Merlot will go well with the blue cheese. Alternatively you could do something a bit different and enjoy an off-dry white; one of the richer Chardonnays would be good.

JUMBO SHRIMP WITH GREMOLATA

Serves 4 as an appetizer or light main course

**Preparation time: 10 minutes
Cooking time: 15 to 20 minutes**

This is an extremely simple way to cook shrimp, and the gremolata garnish really adds a piquant edge. Any of the ribbed skillet grills can be used.

2¼ pounds (1 kg) jumbo shrimp
extra corn oil, for brushing

For the marinade:
½ cup (125 ml) corn oil
½ cup (125 ml) lemon juice
2 garlic cloves, crushed
a little coarse sea salt and freshly
    ground black pepper

For the gremolata:
2 garlic cloves, crushed
2 tablespoons chopped fresh
    flat-leaf parsley
grated zest of 2 lemons
2 tablespoons lemon juice
a little freshly ground black pepper

1 Rinse the shrimp, but do not remove the shells.

2 Mix together the marinade ingredients in a large Le Creuset gratin dish. Add the shrimp and turn them in the marinade. Cover and marinate in the refrigerator for at least 1 hour.

3 Heat the grill over medium heat on the stovetop and brush lightly with oil when it is hot.

4 Drain the shrimp and pat off the excess marinade with paper towels.

5 Add the shrimp to the hot grill and grill for 2 to 3 minutes each side until they are evenly pink; then transfer to a warm serving dish.

6 Mix together all the gremolata ingredients and sprinkle evenly over the cooked shrimp. Serve immediately.

 Alternatively, use a brunch griddle or iron-handle skillet for this recipe.

 The gremolata goes well as a garnish with almost any grilled fish.

 A full-bodied white wine such as an American Pinot Blanc will work well with this dish. In hot weather, try a refreshing, high acidity Rosé such as a Vin Gris or a Tavel.

SEARED TUNA SALAD

Serves 4 as a main course, or 8 as an appetizer

Preparation time: 15 minutes + 15 minutes for the potatoes

Cooking time: 8 to 10 minutes

A ribbed skillet grill is the ideal piece of Le Creuset cookware to use for this recipe, because it produces the flavorsome and decorative "sear" lines.

four 6 ounce (175 g) tuna steaks
a little olive oil
a little coarse sea salt and freshly ground black pepper

For the salad dressing:

finely grated zest of 1 lemon
2 tablespoons lemon juice
4 tablespoons olive oil
1 teaspoon coarse-grain mustard
1 tablespoon fresh chopped flat-leaf parsley
a little salt and freshly ground black pepper

For the salad:

crisp salad leaves
8 ounces (225 g) cherry tomatoes, halved
12 ounces (350 g) cooked new potatoes, cut into ½-inch (1 cm) dice
1 firm avocado, diced
12 pitted black olives

To serve:

crusty bread

1 Brush both sides of the tuna with the oil and season well.

2 Heat the grill over a medium heat on the stovetop and lightly brush with oil when it is hot. Add the tuna steaks and grill for 2 to 3 minutes on each side until they are cooked through. Remove the tuna from the pan and set aside to cool for a few minutes.

3 To make the dressing, put all the ingredients into a bowl and whisk together.

4 To make the salad, tear the salad leaves into bite-size pieces and mix with the other salad ingredients. Transfer to a large shallow bowl or plate and drizzle with three-quarters of the dressing.

5 Using a sharp knife, cut the tuna steaks into strips and lay these over the salad. Drizzle with the remaining dressing and serve with plenty of crusty bread.

 An iron-handle skillet, frypan or the base of a buffet casserole can also be used for this recipe.

 Salmon fillets or thick slices of monkfish can also be used in this recipe.

 A crisp, wood-aged Sauvignon Blanc will work well with this salad. Look for white Bordeaux or a white Meritage style. A Rosé from Bandol or Tavel is another good option.

GRILLED TROPICAL FRUIT WITH RASPBERRY SAUCE

Serves 6

Preparation time: 15 minutes

Cooking time: 5 minutes for the sauce, 10 to 15 minutes for the fruit

This recipe can be cooked all year round and can bring a real sense of sunshine to even the coldest of days. In warm weather it does, of course, make the ideal dessert for cooking outdoors on the barbecue. Indoors, this recipe can be cooked on any ribbed grill or skillet grill.

1 large, firm mango
3 firm bananas
2 tablespoons lemon juice
1 small, firm pineapple
2 tablespoons light brown sugar
2 tablespoons shredded coconut

For the raspberry sauce:

8 ounces (225 g) fresh or frozen
   raspberries, thawed if frozen
2 teaspoons lemon juice
2 tablespoons confectioners' sugar

To serve:

ice cream

1 Make the sauce before cooking the fruits. Put the raspberries into a saucepan, add the lemon juice and sugar, and bring to a boil. Reduce the heat and simmer for 2 minutes. Leave the raspberries to cool, then push them through a strainer to make a purée. Taste and add a little more sugar if necessary.

2 To prepare the fruit, peel the mango, cut the flesh away from the seed and cut it into ½-inch (1 cm) thick slices; do not worry if they are uneven.

3 Peel the bananas and cut them in half crossways; drizzle with the lemon juice.

4 Peel the pineapple and cut the flesh into ½-inch (1 cm) thick rings, removing the tough core.

5 Sprinkle all the fruit with a mixture of the sugar and coconut.

6 Heat the grill over medium heat on the stovetop and brush it with oil when it is hot. Add the fruit and grill for 1 to 2 minutes on each side: take care the fruit does not overcook and become soft. Serve warm with the raspberry sauce and ice cream.

 The grill surface will be sticky after cooking this recipe. Leave the grill to cool for 5 minutes but do not let it cool completely. Fill it with warm water or leave it to soak in warm water for 10 to 15 minutes, then scrub between the ribs with a stiff nylon brush. Wash, rinse, and dry in the normal way.

MULTI-FUNCTION PAN

When the label "multi-function" is given to a piece of equipment it can, in some instances, raise a question mark about the "functionality" of the "multi".

Can it do one thing well and the rest in a very mediocre fashion; or because it is "multi", do none of its functions very well at all; or, does it do a variety of functions really well? For me the multi-function pan (or Marmitout as it is also known) falls very easily into the latter category and can actually live up to its name.

It is a two-part piece: a saucepan base with an integral iron handle and an omelette-size skillet which fits neatly on top as a lid. The two pieces can be used individually, or together, therefore offering a wide choice of use. This may be particularly useful if your kitchen is small and storage space for pans is at a premium. It may also be useful if, as a student, you have to cook yourself an occasional meal on a tiny stovetop. If you are a camper, it's always a bonus to have cooking equipment that can provide a variety of meals and keep the food hot.

So how does this piece live up to its "multi-functional" status? Using the saucepan base and skillet lid together you have a saucepan with a well-fitting lid. The same base and skillet lid can also be used in the oven, when it becomes a casserole or braising dish with all the attributes cast iron has to offer for these recipes. By itself, the base can be used as an open boiling pan while the skillet cooks a sauce, an omelette, a steak or simply fries some eggs. The skillet also makes a handy gratin, baking or roasting dish and can be used under the broiler or in the oven. It can also be used on the stovetop for cooking a meat sauce or vegetables. As with a number of other Le Creuset shapes, the multi-function pan has iron handles on both the saucepan and skillet. This, of course, allows both to be transferred from the stovetop to the oven or the broiler, but care should be taken to handle these at all times with a heatproof oven mitt.

The recipes in this chapter offer a few ideas from which you can expand your own multi-function uses. There are three sizes of multi-function pans; the smallest, 1 quart (18 cm), is ideal for 1 or 2 people, the larger 2 quart (22 cm) for 2 or 3 people, and the largest 3 quart (26 cm) for 3 or 4 people.

General Tip

- These pieces should be used in the same way as all other Le Creuset shapes. Refer to the general tips sections of saucepans and skillets for more detailed information.

SOLE AND SCALLOP ROLL-UPS WITH VERMOUTH SAUCE

Serves 3
Preparation time: 15 minutes
Cooking time: 25 minutes

This recipe is simple to make, but sophisticated enough to serve as an appetizer for a special dinner party. Alternatively, serve it with rice and a green vegetable as a main course. This recipe uses the 2-quart (22 cm) multi-function pan.

For the fish:
6 fillets of lemon sole, skinned
6 sea scallops, shucked
½ cup (125 ml) vermouth
a few sprigs of fresh fennel
a few sprigs fresh flat-leaf parsley
1 bay leaf
salt and freshly ground black
  pepper

For the vermouth sauce:
1 tablespoon butter
1 shallot, chopped finely
1 tablespoon all-purpose flour
½ cup (125 ml) milk
1 teaspoon chopped fresh fennel
1 teaspoon chopped fresh parsley
2 tablespoons whipping cream

1 Roll each sole fillet around a scallop. Secure with a toothpick. Stand the rolls on end in the skillet lid. Add the vermouth, herbs and seasonings.

Cover with a piece of buttered aluminum foil and poach gently on the stovetop for 10 to 12 minutes or until the fish and scallops are tender right through. Carefully drain off the fish cooking liquor into a bowl, discarding the herbs. Cover the fish and keep hot.

2 While the fish is cooking, begin the sauce. Melt the butter in the pan, add the shallot and fry gently until very soft but not colored.

Add the flour and cook until all the butter is absorbed. Remove the pan from the heat.

3 Make up the fish cooking liquor to 1 cup (250 ml) with the milk. Gradually stir this into the cooked roux. Return the pan to the heat and cook, stirring continuously, until thickened. Add the herbs and finally the cream. Do not allow to boil again once the cream is added. Taste and adjust the seasoning.

4 Remove the toothpicks from the fish and pour the sauce over them. Serve from the skillet.

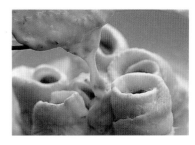

 The same recipe could be cooked in the 1¼-quart (23 cm) skillet and 2¾-quart (20 cm) round French oven.

 This recipe can also be made using flounder fillets.
  Low-fat cream can also be used.

 A white Rhone wine from Hermitage or Chateauneuf-du-Pape will provide an interesting match for this dish or try the Viognier-based wines of Condrieu and Chateau Grillet with their wonderful aromatics.

SPAGHETTI WITH SEAFOOD AND SPINACH SAUCE

Serves 2
Preparation time: 10 minutes
Cooking time: 15 minutes

This is an extremely quick but tasty pasta dish. Using both pieces of the multi-function pan side by side it can be cooked and on the table in minutes. This recipe uses the 2-quart (22 cm) multi-function pan.

6 ounces (175 g) dried spaghetti
a little olive oil

For the seafood and spinach sauce:

1 tablespoon olive oil
1 shallot, chopped finely
1 garlic clove, crushed
8 ounces (225 g) canned crushed
   tomatoes with their juice
½ cup (125 ml) dry white wine
1 tablespoon fresh chopped
   flat-leaf parsley
12 torn fresh basil leaves
6 ounces (175 g) sea scallops,
   cut into bite-size pieces
4½ ounces (125 g) young spinach
   leaves, torn into bite-size pieces
salt and freshly ground black
   pepper

1 To make the sauce, heat the oil in the skillet lid over medium heat. Add the shallot and garlic and fry gently for 2 to 3 minutes until both begin to soften, but not brown.

2 Add the tomatoes with their juice, the wine, parsley, basil, and some seasoning and simmer uncovered for 10 minutes.

3 While the sauce is cooking, cook the spaghetti in the multi-function pan in plenty of boiling, salted water with a little olive oil, until it is "al dente". Drain well.

4 When the sauce has simmered for 10 minutes, stir in the scallops and the spinach leaves. Cook for 3 to 5 minutes longer until the scallops are cooked through and opaque, and the spinach has wilted into the sauce. Taste and adjust the seasoning.

5 Return the cooked spaghetti to the multi-function pan and stir the sauce gently through it, taking care not to break up the scallops. Serve immediately.

 A 2-quart (20 cm) saucepan and small skillet can also be used for this recipe.

 Other firm fish such as cod or monkfish can be used in this sauce instead of the scallops.

 Try an Italian white wine with the pasta – either an Orvieto Arneis or Soave will work well.

BEEF GOULASH WITH CARAWAY POTATOES

Serves 4
Preparation time: 25 minutes
Cooking time: 40 minutes

Goulash is an internationally-famous Hungarian beef stew flavored with paprika. This recipe uses ground beef and the caraway potatoes provide an alternative accompaniment to the usual ribbon noodles or plain boiled potatoes. The 3-quart (26 cm) multi-function pan is used for this recipe.

For the caraway potatoes:

1 pound (450 g) boiling potatoes
¼ cup (60 ml) vegetable oil
1 small onion, sliced thinly
2 garlic cloves, crushed
¼ teaspoon caraway seeds
a pinch of salt and ground black
   pepper

For the goulash:

2 tablespoons vegetable oil
1 medium onion, chopped roughly
1 green bell pepper, seeded and
   chopped
1 pound (450 g) lean ground beef
2 teaspoons all-purpose flour
4 teaspoons paprika
2 tablespoons tomato paste
1 pound (450 g) canned crushed
   tomatoes with their juice
a pinch of salt
½ cup (125 ml) sour cream, to
   garnish

1 Cut the potatoes into ½-inch (1 cm) thick slices. Put them into the multi-function pan and cover with water, adding a little salt. Bring to the boil, cover with the skillet lid and boil for 4 to 5 minutes until they are "just" tender. Drain well and rinse with cold water. Put to one side.

2 Rinse and dry the pan and skillet lid. To make the goulash, heat the 2 tablespoons of oil in the pan over a medium heat on the stovetop. Fry the onions and bell pepper until both are beginning to soften. Add the ground beef and fry, stirring occasionally until it is beginning to brown.

3 Stir in all the remaining ingredients for the goulash except the sour cream. Cover with the skillet lid, lower the heat and simmer gently for 30 minutes. Remove the skillet lid and dry. Leave the goulash over a very low heat to keep hot.

4 Heat the oil for the potatoes in the skillet. Add the onion and fry for one minute before adding the garlic and potatoes. Fry, stirring occasionally, until the potatoes and onions are a light golden brown. Stir in the caraway seeds and a little pepper.

5 To serve, place a portion of the goulash beside a portion of the potatoes, topping the goulash with a little sour cream as a garnish.

A round 3½-quart (22 cm) French oven and a skillet or frypan can also be used for this recipe.

Ground pork or turkey can also be used. If sour cream is not available, use heavy cream and add 2 teaspoons of lemon juice to it.

BUTTERMILK PANCAKES WITH CHERRY AND MASCARPONE TOPPING

Makes twelve 5-inch (13 cm) pancakes
Preparation time: 15 minutes
Cooking time: 15 minutes

The cherry topping can be left simmering while you cook the pancakes. The mascarpone cheese makes a lovely combination with the cherries, but ice cream is just as good. The skillet lid of the 2-quart (22 cm) multi-function pan is just the right size to use for making these pancakes.

For the pancake batter:

1¼ cups (175 g) sifted all-purpose flour
4 tablespoons white sugar
1 teaspoon baking powder
½ teaspoon salt
½ teaspoon baking soda
1 cup (250 ml) buttermilk
½ cup (125 ml) milk
3 tablespoons (45 g) butter, melted
2 large eggs
vegetable oil, for cooking

For the cherry topping:

1 pound (450 g) canned pitted black cherries
1 tablespoon white sugar
finely grated zest of 1 lemon
2 teaspoons cornstarch
8 ounces (225 g) mascarpone cheese

1 Sift all the dry ingredients for the pancake batter into a bowl. Make a well in the middle.

2 Beat together all the wet ingredients except the vegetable oil, and gradually add these to the flour, beating between additions. Leave the batter to stand while preparing the cherry topping.

3 To make the topping, drain the cherries, reserving the juice. Put the cherries, sugar, lemon zest, and 4 tablespoons of the reserved cherry juice into the multi-function pan over a medium heat and bring to a boil, stirring. Blend the cornstarch with a little water and stir into the cherries, reduce the heat, and simmer until the sauce thickens.

4 To cook the pancakes, heat 1 tablespoon of vegetable oil in the skillet lid. When it is hot, wipe the excess oil out of the pan with paper towels. Pour about ¼ cup (3 tablespoons) of the batter into the pan and cook until bubbles break through the top surface. Using a pancake turner or metal spatula, turn the pancake over and

cook the other side. Keep warm on a plate loosely covered with aluminum foil while you cook the remaining batter. Wipe the pan surface with oiled paper towel between pancakes.

5 To serve, spoon a little of the cherry sauce over one half of a pancake and put a spoonful of mascarpone cheese on the other half. Serve immediately.

 A 2-quart (20 cm) saucepan and small skillet can also be used for this recipe.

 For a little luxury, add 2 tablespoons cherry brandy to the sauce.
  These pancakes make a good basic base for any

topping or filling, or they can be topped with scrambled eggs. Do not add the sugar for savory pancakes.

CHICKEN LIVERS WITH WILD RICE PILAU

Serves 2 or 3

Preparation time: 15 minutes

Cooking time: 25 minutes for the pilau, 10 minutes for the chicken livers

Chicken livers are a good "stand-by" ingredient to have in the freezer, because they can be thawed quickly. In this recipe they are combined with fresh sage and sour cream, both of which slightly offset the "sweetness" the livers have. The accompanying wild rice pilau goes particularly well with the livers, but you can also serve them with plain rice or noodles. The 2-quart (22 cm) multi-function pan is used for this recipe.

8 ounces (225 g) chicken livers,
    trimmed of sinews
½ cup (125 ml) milk
¼ cup (60 g) finely chopped bacon
1 tablespoon olive oil
1 shallot, chopped finely
1 cup (70 g) button mushrooms,
    halved
12 fresh sage leaves, chopped
½ cup (125 ml) sour cream
fresh parsley leaves, to garnish

For the pilau:
¼ cup (50 g) wild rice
1 tablespoon olive oil
1 shallot, chopped finely

½ cup (100 g) long-grain rice
1½ cups (375 ml) hot chicken stock
1 tablespoon fresh chopped
    parsley
¼ cup (40 g) raisins
2 tablespoons pine nuts
salt and freshly ground black
    pepper

1 To make the pilau, put the wild rice in the multi-function pan with 2 cups (500 ml) water over high heat and bring to a boil. Reduce the heat and simmer for 25 minutes. Drain the rice and rinse with cold water. Wash and dry the pan.

2 While the wild rice is cooking, rinse the chicken livers well. Cut them into bite-size pieces, place in a bowl, and cover with the milk; leave to stand for 10 to 15 minutes.

3 Heat the oil for the pilau in the pan over medium heat. Add the shallot and fry gently until it begins to soften, but not brown. Add the wild and long-grain rices, stirring so they absorb the oil.

4 Stir in the hot stock with the parsley and some seasoning.

Simmer for 20 minutes, stirring occasionally.

5 While the rice is cooking, cook the livers. Drain and pat them dry with paper towels. Heat the skillet lid over medium heat. Add the bacon and cook slowly until the fat begins to run. Add the oil and shallot and continue frying for 1 to 2 minutes until the shallot is soft.

6 Add the livers and fry, stirring, until they are evenly brown and just cooked through; do not overcook or they will become tough. Stir in the mushrooms, sage leaves, and some seasoning and continue cooking for 1 minute longer.

7 Stir in the sour cream and turn off the heat. Stir for just a few seconds to warm the cream and coat the chicken livers.

8 Stir the raisins and pine nuts into the pilau.

9 Serve the pilau on warm plates with the chicken livers piled on top, garnished with a few parsley leaves.

 A 2-quart (20 cm) saucepan and a small skillet can also be used for this recipe.

 Calves' liver can also be used in this recipe. Soaking the livers in milk helps to plump them and mellow the flavor.

If you don't have any sour cream, use ½ cup (125 ml) heavy cream with 2 teaspoons of lemon juice added.

CHICKEN IN CIDER SAUCE WITH APPLE RINGS

Serves 6
Preparation time: 15 minutes
Cooking time: 35 minutes

This recipe is based on a traditional dish called "Poulet Vallée d'Auge" from the Normandy region of France. It makes use of some of the main produce from that area, namely hard apple cider, Calvados apple brandy, and crème fraîche. The 3-quart (26 cm) multi-function pan is ideal for this recipe.

3 dessert apples, peeled and cored
5 tablespoons (75 g) unsalted butter
1½ cups (125 g) firm, sliced mushrooms
6 boned and skinned chicken breast halves
1 cup (250 ml) hard apple cider
2 tablespoons Calvados apple brandy
4 tablespoons crème fraîche or sour cream
salt and freshly ground black pepper

1 Take one of the prepared apples and chop it finely. Cover the other two apples with cold water to prevent discoloration. Heat half of the butter in the multi-function pan over medium heat. Add the chopped apple and fry it slowly, stirring, until it begins to soften and color. Add the mushrooms and continue cooking for 1 minute longer. Using a slotted spoon, lift out the apple and mushrooms, draining well.

2 Cut the chicken breast pieces into long, finger-size strips. Fry a few of these at a time in the hot butter remaining in the pan until they are all brown. Return the apple and mushrooms to the pan with the cider and some seasoning. Cover with the skillet lid and simmer for 20 to 25 minutes until the chicken is tender.

3 Remove the lid and wipe dry to use for frying the apple rings. Use the slotted spoon to remove the chicken, mushrooms, and apple from the pan and transfer them to a warm serving dish. Keep hot. Melt the remaining butter in the skillet lid. Cut the remaining apples into thick slices and dry them on paper towels. Fry them until pale golden brown on both sides.

4 While the apple rings are cooking, return the multi-function pan to a high heat and boil the liquid hard for several minutes to reduce by one-third. Stir in the Calvados and crème fraîche or sour cream. Taste and adjust the seasoning before pouring over the chicken. Garnish with the apple rings and serve immediately.

 A 3½-quart (22 cm) round French oven and a skillet can also be used for this recipe.

 If Calvados is difficult to find, use Cognac or Applejack.
Heavy cream can be used instead of the crème fraîche, but add 1 teaspoon of lemon juice to the sauce to sharpen the flavor.

AU GRATIN DISHES

A crisp-topped seafood gratin or a traditional potato dauphinois with crunchy pieces of potato around the edge is difficult to resist and you will often hear guests say that they really enjoy "the slightly overcooked bits". The term "au gratin" literally means, "burnt on top" but, thankfully, most recipes will stop short of being burnt and just be nicely browned and crisp.

Gratins are meant to be served from the dish in which they are cooked, and with their elegant shape and heat-retaining qualities, Le Creuset gratin dishes really are the ideal "cook-and-serve" dishes. Many recipes, such as the Potato Dauphinois on page 73, can be prepared in advance, chilled and then baked as required, which is a great time-saver when entertaining. Their design is intentional. The wide shallow shape allows plenty of surface area to become quickly browned while the food underneath stays moist. The shallow shape and the "eared" handles of a Le Creuset gratin dish are very recognisable and this shape allows them to go under the broiler or in the top of the oven when you are cooking many other dishes.

Since they are made from cast iron, they can be put directly on the stovetop. This is particularly helpful when melting ingredients as part of a recipe such as the Pineapple Upside-down Cake on page 70. Gratin dishes in other materials do not have the same durability and flexibility of use. In addition to being ideal for gratin recipes, these dishes can be used for a vast array of things: baking whole fish, roasting chicken pieces, or baking chops. The dish can then, of course, be taken straight to the table which reduces the risk of breaking up the food before it is served.

Marinating food is as much a part of my food preparation as chopping vegetables; even the simplest of meats can be transformed with a few marinade ingredients and gratin dishes are ideal for marinating. The porcelain enamel surface is non-reactive, so it will not stain or absorb flavors and will not be damaged by acidic ingredients such as lemon juice or wine. The shape is wide so foods can often be put in one layer allowing them to be coated evenly in the marinade. If necessary, it is also possible to rinse the gratin dish after marinating and use it for cooking and serving too.

Another use I discovered some years ago for the gratin dish was for baking pies, tarts and quiches. For those who cook these recipes regularly the term "soggy bottom", referring to the underside of a piecrust which is wet and undercooked, will ring bells; there is nothing worse than a crisp crust edge that disappears into a chewy grey center. To say that it never happens with cast iron would be overstating the case, but in my long experience of cooking with many, many materials, piecrusts baked in cast iron dishes are probably the crispest and most reliable you will ever bake. Two recipes, the Cheese and Asparagus Quiche on page 74 and Baked Raisin Cheesecake on page 75, illustrate the point perfectly. There is no need to pre-bake the piecrust before filling with the wet ingredients; the evenness and efficiency of the heat absorption into the cast iron makes this unnecessary.

Cakes and desserts are also beautifully cooked, the cast iron giving a very gentle but even rise to the mixture as it bakes. These can be turned out very easily when the dish has been lightly greased and floured before use.

The recipes begin with a step-by-step guide for making Pineapple Upside-down Cake. This is followed by some of my favorite recipes for gratin dishes. There are two sizes of oval gratin dish, the 1½ quart (28 cm) and the 2⅞ quart (36 cm). There are also individual portion petite au gratins, which make perfect cook-and-serve dishes for appetizers and desserts.

General Tips

- When making a gratin recipe, fill the dish almost to the brim so that the top will crisp and brown quickly and evenly. In this way the food beneath will not dry out.
- Grease the dish for all gratins so that the foods release easily and the dish is easier to wash.
- Always use medium or low heats when placing the gratin dish on the stovetop for melting or frying ingredients.
- When using the dish for pastry there is no need to grease the dish. There will be sufficient fat in the pastry to prevent it from sticking to the porcelain enamel surface.
- There is no need to brush the surface of raw or cooked pastry shells with egg to seal the surface and prevent soggy pastry.
- Always grease and flour the surface when using the dish for cake mixtures. If it is a delicate cake, put a piece of baking parchment paper in the base as well.
- Always use a round bladed (not sharp) knife for easing around the sides of the dish or for cutting foods in the dish. Hard pressure using a sharp knife will eventually damage the porcelain enamel.
- Allow all pastry and cake recipes to cool in the dish for at least 10 minutes before turning out. In this way the cast iron will have cooled sufficiently to make handling easier. However, a cloth or oven mitts may still be required to hold the handles.
- When taking a hot gratin dish straight to the table do ensure that it is placed on a good heatproof mat. The dish will stay hot for some considerable time.

PINEAPPLE UPSIDE-DOWN CAKE

Serves 6 to 8
Preparation time: 20 minutes
Cooking time: 30 to 35 minutes

This recipe takes full advantage of the way in which a gratin dish can be used: directly on the stovetop and in the oven. It is a recipe that can be served hot as a dessert with ice cream, or it makes a delicious, moist cake for cutting. The 11-inch (28 cm) oval gratin dish is used for this recipe.

4 tablespoons or ½ stick (60 g) butter, diced
⅓ cup (60 g) light brown sugar
1 pound (450 g) canned pineapple slices, drained
12 candied cherries

For the cake batter:
¾ cup (175 g) superfine granulated sugar
1½ sticks (175 g) butter or margarine, softened
1⅓ cups (175 g) self-rising flour
1 teaspoon baking powder
3 large eggs

1 Put the diced butter in the gratin dish over medium heat on the stovetop and melt. Swirl the butter around the dish so a little of the butter greases the sides. Return the gratin dish to the heat, sprinkle the light brown sugar evenly over the bottom and leave for just a few seconds to melt the sugar.

2 Preheat the oven to 325°F/160°C/Gas Mark 3. Remove the dish from the heat and arrange a pattern of the halved pineapple slices and cherries over the bottom, pushing them close together.

3 Put all the ingredients for the cake batter into a food processor and process for 10 to 20 seconds until the batter is smooth. Drop several spoonfuls of the batter over the fruit to hold it in place, then add the remainder, spreading evenly.

4 Bake the cake in the middle of the oven for 30 to 35 minutes until it is well risen, golden brown, and springs back when lightly touched. Leave the cake to cool in the dish for at least 10 minutes before unmolding. Ease around the sides of the cake with a round-bladed knife or metal spatula before inverting it onto a wide, shallow plate for serving.

 A 10-inch (26 cm) iron-handle skillet can also be used for this recipe.

 The cake can also be made as a one-step batter in a bowl. Use an electric mixer or spoon to beat all the batter ingredients until smooth.
Canned or fresh apricots or

peaches can be used in this recipe instead of pineapple.
If the cake cools before it is unmolded, reheat the sugar and butter in the bottom by standing the dish over low heat for just a few seconds.

ZUCCHINI AND CARROT GRATIN

Serves 6 to 8

Preparation time: 20 minutes

Cooking time: 20 to 25 minutes

This makes a tasty vegetarian meal or can be used as a side vegetable dish with meats and poultry. The 11-inch (28 cm) oval gratin dish is used for this recipe.

2 tablespoons olive oil
3 cups (350 g) coarsely grated
　zucchini
2 cups (250 g) coarsely grated
　carrots
1 medium onion, chopped finely
4 large eggs, beaten
1 cup (250 ml) whipping cream
1 cup (125 g) coarsely grated
　Gruyère cheese
1 tablespoon fresh chopped
　parsley
½ teaspoon ground nutmeg
2 tablespoons sesame seeds
salt and freshly ground black
　pepper

1 Preheat the oven to 350°F/180°C/Gas Mark 4. Heat the oil in a large, nonstick frypan over a medium heat on the stovetop. Add all the vegetables and turn them around in the hot oil until they are just beginning to soften. Remove the pan from the heat.

2 Beat together the eggs, cream, cheese, parsley, nutmeg, and plenty of seasoning. Pour this over the vegetables, stirring well.

3 Transfer the mixture into the well-greased gratin dish, levelling the top. Scatter the sesame seeds evenly over the vegetables.

4 Bake in the middle of the oven for 20 to 25 minutes until the gratin is just firm to the touch and pale golden brown on top.

 If you have the 14-inch (36 cm) version, increase the quantity of all the ingredients by half. The basic recipe can also be made in the 10-inch (26 cm) iron-handle skillet.

 If there are any leftovers, cut them into portions and fry lightly in olive oil to serve at another meal.

POTATO DAUPHINOIS

Serves 8 to 10

Preparation time: 25 minutes

Cooking time: 40 to 45 minutes + parboiling the potatoes

In France this dish is called "gratin dauphinois". It is an excellent potato dish for a large family gathering or a celebration meal because it is flexible and can be prepared in advance up to the end of Step 4, to be baked when required. Waxy potatoes give the best result because they hold their shape. The 14-inch (36 cm) oval gratin dish is used for this recipe.

3 pounds 5 ounces (1.5 kg) waxy
    potatoes, peeled
1 large garlic clove, halved
1 tablespoon (15 g) butter,
    softened
¼ teaspoon ground nutmeg
1 cup (125 g) finely grated Gruyère
    cheese
1 cup (250 ml) heavy cream
½ cup (125 ml) milk
salt and freshly ground black
    pepper

1 Cut the potatoes into ¼-inch (5 mm) slices. Put them into a large French oven or saucepan on the stovetop, cover with cold water and a little salt, and bring to a boil on a high heat. Reduce the heat and simmer for 2 minutes. Do not overcook at this stage because even waxy potatoes can begin to break up; drain well.

2 Rub the inside of the gratin dish with the cut garlic and grease with a little of the butter.

3 Preheat the oven to 325°F/160°C/Gas Mark 3. Put half the potatoes into the dish, spreading them evenly. Sprinkle with a little of the nutmeg and some seasoning. Add half the cheese and then another layer of potatoes, nutmeg, and seasonings.

4 Beat together the cream and the milk and pour evenly over the potatoes. Finish by scattering the remaining cheese on top with a few small pieces of butter dotted over the surface.

5 Bake in the middle of the oven for 40 to 45 minutes until a deep crisp brown crust forms. Serve immediately from the dish.

This recipe can also be baked in the 12-inch (30 cm) iron-handle skillet.

Low-fat cream and milk can be used in this recipe, and the Gruyère can be replaced with a low-fat cheese such as Cheddar.

CHEESE AND ASPARAGUS QUICHE

Serves 6 to 8

**Preparation time: 10 minutes
for the piecrust dough,
5 minutes for the filling**

**Cooking time: 35 to 40
minutes**

*A good quiche makes the ideal
dish for a picnic, buffet, or any
casual entertaining with your family
or friends. In this recipe the cheese
flavor is enhanced by adding it to
the crust as well as the filling. Try
my method of making the dough
with milk; it makes a very light,
crisp texture. This recipe uses the
11-inch (28 cm) oval gratin.*

For the piecrust:

1⅓ cups (175 g) all-purpose flour
½ teaspoon salt
5 tablespoons or ¾ stick (75 g)
    cold butter, diced
½ cup (60 g) finely grated sharp
    Cheddar cheese
1½ to 2 tablespoons milk

For the filling:

1½ cups (175 g) finely grated sharp
    Cheddar cheese
1 pound (450 g) canned
    asparagus spears, drained and
    chopped

4 large eggs
1 cup (250 ml) heavy cream
1½ teaspoons Dijon mustard
a little salt and freshly ground black
    pepper

1 Put the flour, salt, and butter
into a bowl. Using your fingertips,
or a pastry blender, work the butter
into the flour until it resembles
coarse bread crumbs. Stir in the
cheese and milk, working it into a
dough.

2 Turn out the dough on to a
floured surface and knead gently
until it is smooth. Wrap in plastic
wrap and leave to stand at room
temperature for 30 minutes to 1
hour.

3 Roll out the dough on a
floured surface until it is large
enough to line the bottom and
sides of the dish. Carefully press it
into the dish, trimming the top level
with the top of the dish. Cover and
chill for at least 1 hour.

4 Preheat the oven to
375°F/190°C/Gas Mark 5. To
make the filling, spread half the
cheese over the dough-lined
gratin dish. Add a layer of the
asparagus, reserving a few of the
best tips for the garnish. Add the
remaining cheese.

5 Beat the eggs, cream, and
mustard with a little salt and
pepper. Pour this over the filling
and use the reserved asparagus
tips to garnish the top.

6 Bake in the middle of
the oven for 20 minutes, then
reduce the temperature to
325°F/160°C/Gas Mark 3 and
continue cooking for 15 to 20
minutes longer, or until the filling
is set and the top pale golden
brown.

7 Leave to cool for 10 to 15
minutes before serving, because a
quiche is at its best when warm,
not piping hot.

*To make a larger quiche, use
the 14-inch (36 cm) oval
gratin and increase
the quantity of all the
ingredients by half.*

*Store-bought piecrust dough
can be used for this recipe.
When rolling out the dough
scatter it with the cheese so it
gets pressed in. Proceed from
Step 3.*

*Resting and chilling the dough
prevents it from being overstretched so
it doesn't "shrink" dramatically when it
goes in the hot oven.*

*Low-fat dairy products can be used
in this recipe.*

BAKED RAISIN CHEESECAKE

Serves 6 to 8

Preparation time: 30 minutes

Cooking time: about 35 minutes

This is based on a very traditional recipe. I first baked it many years ago in a Le Creuset gratin dish for a trade fair in Germany and it has acquired quite a following since. The raisins can be omitted altogether, if preferred, or replaced with currants or candied citrus peel. This recipe uses the 11-inch (28 cm) oval gratin.

6 ounces (175 g) store-bought
  piecrust dough
2 sticks (225 g) butter, softened
1 cup (225 g) superfine granulated
  sugar
4 large eggs, beaten
finely grated zest of 2 lemons
two 8-ounce packs (2 x 250 g)
  cream cheese, pressed though
  a strainer
6 tablespoons lemon juice
½ cup (60 g) raisins

To finish:

1 teaspoon superfine granulated
  sugar
a pinch of ground cinnamon

1 On a floured surface, roll out the dough so it is large enough to line the bottom and sides of the dish. Carefully press the dough into the dish, trimming the top level with the top of the dish. Cover and chill for at least 1 hour.

2 Preheat the oven to 400°F/200°C/Gas Mark 6. Beat together the butter and sugar until light and fluffy. Add the eggs, a little at a time, then stir in the lemon zest.

3 Beat in the cream cheese, lemon juice, and raisins. Pour this batter into the dough-lined dish.

4 Bake in the middle of the heated oven for 15 minutes, then reduce to 350°F/180°C/Gas Mark 4 and continue baking for 20 minutes longer, or until the crust is golden and the filling set. Set aside to cool completely. Before serving, dust the sugar and cinnamon on the top.

 The Le Creuset Tatin dish can also be used for this recipe.

 If you are making the piecrust dough, use 1⅓ cups (175 g) all-purpose flour, ¾ stick (75 g) chilled butter with a pinch of salt and 1½ to 2 tablespoons of cold water.

Low-fat butter and cream cheese can be used in this recipe.

Baked Jumbo Shrimp and Scallops in Cream

Serves 6

Preparation time: 20 minutes

Cooking time: 10 to 12 minutes

When you are entertaining, it is so helpful if some of the dishes can be prepared in advance, ready to be cooked when guests arrive. This is just such a recipe. If anything, I think the flavor improves when it is left to rest for a few hours. This recipe uses six petite au gratin dishes.

2 pounds 4 ounces (1 kg) shelled
    raw jumbo shrimp
12 large sea scallops, shucked
1½ cups (375 ml) heavy cream
1 tablespoon fresh chopped
    flat-leaf parsley
salt and freshly ground black
    pepper

For the topping:
2 cups (125 g) fresh white bread
    crumbs
1 tablespoon fresh chopped
    flat-leaf parsley
½ teaspoon cayenne pepper
4 tablespoons finely grated fresh
    parmesan cheese

1 Rinse and pat dry the shrimp and scallops.

2 Preheat the oven to 350°F/180°C/Gas Mark 4. Arrange a few of the shrimp in each of the au gratin dishes. Cut each scallop into 3 pieces and push these between the shrimp, dividing them equally.

3 Mix together the cream, parsley, salt and pepper. Divide this mixture equally between the dishes.

4 Mix together the topping ingredients. Scatter equally over the tops so all the seafood is covered.

5 Bake for 10 to 12 minutes, or until the cream is bubbling at the edges and the topping pale golden brown. Serve hot.

 The same volume of ingredients can be cooked in the 11-inch (28 cm) au gratin dish, and served from the dish.

 If you want to prepare this in advance, follow the recipe until the end of Step 4, then cover each dish with plastic wrap and leave in the refrigerator for up to 6 hours. Bake as given.

 The combination of shellfish and cream in this dish makes it the perfect candidate for a big, full-bodied American Chardonnay. A rich Pinot Blanc will also be a good match.

PEACH AND RASPBERRY CHEESE BRÛLÉE

Serves 6
Preparation time: 20 minutes
Cooking time: 5 to 6 minutes

This version of a brûlée topping is less rich and brittle than the usual recipe, but nevertheless just as good. The recipe uses six petite au gratin dishes.

4 large, ripe, fresh peaches
2 cups (125 g) lightly crushed
   Amaretti cookies
1 cup (125 g) fresh raspberries
a little butter, for greasing
fresh mint sprigs, to decorate
   (optional)

For the topping:

2 cups (500 g) ricotta cheese
1 cup (250 ml) low-fat whipping
   cream
½ teaspoon vanilla extract
2 teaspoons sugar

For the brûlée:

1½ cups (300g) sugar

1 Plunge the peaches into boiling water for 1 minute, then into cold water for 2 minutes. Peel off the skins. Halve each, remove the pit, and cut each half into at least 8 slices.

2 Put a little of the crushed Amaretti cookies over the bottom of each lightly-buttered dish. Cover with a layer of the sliced peaches and raspberries, reserving a few raspberries to decorate the tops.

3 To make the topping, beat together the ricotta cheese, cream, vanilla extract, and sugar. Spread the topping evenly over the fruit in each dish, taking it right up to the edges. Liberally sprinkle the remaining 1½ cups (300 g) sugar for the brûlée over the tops.

4 Place the dishes under a hot broiler until the sugar caramelizes. Watch this process carefully because once the sugar melts, the caramel can quickly burn.

5 Leave to cool thoroughly, then chill for 2 to 3 hours before serving. Decorate the tops with a few of the reserved raspberries and fresh mint leaves, if available.

 The same quantity of ingredients can also be cooked in the 11-inch (28 cm) oval au gratin dish.

 This dessert can be made in advance, but remember, the longer the crisp brûlée topping is left, the softer it will become. Any mixture of soft fruits, such as strawberries and raspberries, works well in this recipe, as do mangoes and nectarines.

A good sturdy roasting dish is indispensable in the kitchen, not least for those times of the year when the over-sized turkey has to be dealt with. If you only roast at times of celebration then, obviously, choose a dish size to fit this occasion, but if you roast throughout the year, choose a dish that will accommodate a smaller joint or bird better. A small joint in a large dish will only cause unnecessary splattering of hot fat making the cleaning of the dish and oven more difficult.

Le Creuset roasting dishes have a number of features that make them ideal for all types of roasts but they also have many other uses too. They make ideal dishes for deep pasta bakes, deep family pies and cakes. The facility to use them on the stovetop opens the way to other recipes too, such as the Lemon Chicken Gratiné on page 80. Here the chicken and other ingredients are browned and softened in the dish on the stovetop before being transferred to the oven to complete cooking.

For roasting, it is an advantage to have the deep sides found on these dishes. These will still allow the degree of crisping and browning you want to achieve, but will also contain much of the fat that will inevitably splatter as the roast cooks. The dish also needs to be sturdy enough not to warp either in the oven or when used on the stovetop. A real bonus when roasting is the facility to drain away the roasting fat then place the dish directly on the stovetop to de-glaze it for a gravy or sauce. In this way, all the flavors accumulated during roasting are not lost and the gravy is much richer as a result.

Because cast iron retains heat so well, roasting temperatures can be achieved and maintained at lower than usual oven temperatures. Whereas you may use 400°F/200°C/Gas Mark 6 for other materials, a cast iron dish seldom requires temperatures over 350°F/180°C/ Gas Mark 4 to achieve the same results. If, however, a recipe does require a short blast at higher temperatures to seal the poultry or joint this will generally be achieved at no higher than 400°F/200°C/Gas Mark 6.

As with all other oven-baking or roasting dishes it is important to allow at least a 2-inch (5 cm) gap all around the dish once it is placed on the oven shelf. In this way the correct flow of hot air in the oven can circulate to give even cooking results.

On the barbecue the dishes make ideal keep-hot containers or cooking dishes. If placed at the side of the barbecue, away from the direct heat, they will absorb sufficient heat to keep cooked meats, ribs, or vegetables piping hot, or they can be placed directly over the coals to cook baked potatoes or corn cobs.

The recipes in this chapter begin with the step-by-step Lemon Chicken Gratiné on page 80 which I have now cooked in a number of countries with huge success. It shows how well the dish adapts from a browning dish on the stovetop to a baking dish in the oven.

The Le Creuset roasters are in two sizes: 2½ quart (30 cm) and a larger 6½ quart (40 cm). The larger dish will cook a 13 to 15 pound (6 to 7 kg) turkey and a recipe is given on page 83.

General Tips

- Choose a roaster size to suit your everyday needs and the size and weight of meat you would normally roast. A small joint in a large dish may roast a little quicker and will cause more fat splattering.
- Lightly oil or grease the dish before roasting.
- A light cover of aluminum foil can be tucked over the rim and handles of the dish. This can sometimes be useful for longer slower roasting when the meat may need a little longer to tenderize. The foil can then be removed to brown and crisp the outside.
- After roasting always drain off any excess fat or oil from the dish before adding the thickener or liquid for the gravy. Always add hot liquid to the hot dish. Stir over a medium heat to thicken the consistency.
- When using the dish for cakes, either grease and flour it, or line with parchment baking paper. There is no need to grease the dish when it is lined with pastry.
- After any use allow the dish to cool for a few minutes before filling with warm water, then allow it to stand for 10 to 15 minutes before washing in the normal way. This makes cleaning very easy and the need to use nylon pan scrubbers almost obsolete.
- Never plunge a hot dish straight from the oven or stovetop into cold water or fill with cold water, as damage to the porcelain enamel may occur.

LEMON CHICKEN GRATINÉ

Serves 6

Preparation time: 15 minutes

Cooking time: about 40 minutes

This tangy, lemon-flavored chicken dish is finished with a crisp bread crumb topping, so it combines a variety of flavors and textures. This recipe demonstrates the real versatility of Le Creuset cookware; the whole recipe – frying, making the sauce, and baking – is all done in one pan and then finally the pan is taken straight to the table. Serve straight from the dish with a green vegetable or crisp salad. This recipe uses the 2½-quart (30 cm) roaster.

6 boned and skinned chicken breast halves
1 tablespoon (15 g) butter, softened
1 tablespoon olive oil
1 small onion, chopped finely
1 garlic clove, crushed
finely grated zest of 3 lemons
2 tablespoons lemon juice
1 tablespoon cornstarch
1 tablespoon fresh chopped cilantro
1 cup (250 ml) hot chicken stock
1 cup (250 ml) heavy cream
1½ cups (75 g) fresh white bread crumbs
salt and freshly ground black pepper
a green vegetable or crisp salad, to serve

1 Cut the chicken into long, finger-size strips. Melt the butter and oil together in the roaster over medium heat on the stovetop. Add the onion and garlic and gently fry without coloring, reducing the heat if the onion begins to brown. Add the chicken strips and brown these evenly on all sides.

2 Preheat the oven to 350°F/180°C/Gas Mark 4. Mix together the zest of 2 lemons with the lemon juice, cornstarch, and three-quarters of the cilantro. Blend this with the hot stock and pour over the chicken, stirring as the sauce thickens.

3 Stir in the cream and season to taste. Remove the roaster from the heat. Mix together the bread crumbs and remaining lemon zest and cilantro and scatter evenly over the top of the chicken.

Transfer to the top of the oven and cook for 15 to 20 minutes, or until the top is crisp and pale golden brown.

 This recipe can also be made in the base of the 2½-quart (26 cm) buffet casserole.

 Strips of turkey breast can also be used in this recipe.
Low-fat butter and cream can be used for a reduced-fat dish.

 Look for a big, full-flavoured Chardonnay with citrus fruit character to accompany this dish.

Seafood Lasagne

Serves 6
Preparation time: 35 minutes
Cooking time: 25 to 30 minutes

Lasagne is one of my favorite pasta dishes, and this recipe has been shared with many family and friends. The seafood can be changed to suit personal taste and what is readily available. This recipe uses the 2½-quart (30 cm) roaster.

6 ounces (175 g) dried lasagne sheets (about 9 sheets)

For the filling:

2¼ pounds (1 kg) cod or other firm white fish
8 ounces (225 g) small shucked scallops
8 ounces (225 g) cooked, shelled small shrimp
4 cups (1 litre) milk
2 bay leaves
3 tablespoons (45 g) butter or margarine, softened
3 tablespoons all-purpose flour
1 teaspoon dried marjoram
1 teaspoon dried parsley
2 tablespoons tomato paste
a pinch of ground nutmeg
2 cups (225 g) coarsely grated sharp Cheddar cheese
salt and freshly ground black pepper

1 Cook the lasagne as directed on the package until it is "al dente": drain and rinse with cold water to stop the cooking. Spread out the sheets on a clean dish towel until required, then cover with plastic wrap so they do not dry out.

2 Put the fish and scallops into the roaster. Add 1 cup (250 ml) of the milk with the bay leaves. Cover with aluminum foil and poach gently on the stovetop for 5 to 8 minutes until both are tender. Leave the fish to cool slightly, then pour off the poaching liquid and reserve for making the sauce. When the fish is cool enough to handle, flake the flesh, removing any small bones. Cut each scallop in half. Wash, dry and grease the roaster well.

3 Melt the butter in a medium-size saucepan over low heat. Stir in the flour and over the same low heat cook, stirring, until the "roux" begins to look pale golden brown in color. Remove the pan from the heat and gradually stir in the milk, including the reserved poaching liquid.

4 Return the pan to a medium heat and bring to the boil, stirring continuously. Reduce the heat again and simmer, stirring, for 2 to 3 minutes.

5 Stir in the herbs, tomato paste, nutmeg, and plenty of seasoning, together with three-quarters of the cheese, and continue simmering until the cheese melts.

6 Preheat the oven to 350°F/180°C/Gas Mark 4. Grease the roaster well. Spread 6 tablespoons of the sauce over the bottom of the roaster, then add one-third of the lasagne sheets. Add half the fish, scallops, and shrimp, and season well.

7 Repeat these layers once more. Cover with the last of the lasagne sheets and the remaining sauce. Scatter the remaining cheese over the top.

8 Bake in the oven for 25 to 30 minutes until the sauce is bubbling and the top golden brown.

 To make a much larger quantity for a party, use the 16-inch (40 cm) roaster, doubling all the ingredients.

 Fresh herbs can be used when available. Use 1 tablespoon each of the fresh herbs.
Poached fresh salmon is also very good in this recipe.

Skim milk and low-fat cheese can also be used.

ROASTED STUFFED BELL PEPPERS

Serves 6 as a side vegetable, 3 as a main course

Preparation time: 15 minutes

Cooking time: 45 to 50 minutes

Roasting vegetables, such as bell peppers, has probably been one of the fastest growing trends in cooking over recent years. We are all encouraged to eat more fresh vegetables, and this is a delicious way to do so. This recipe uses the 2½-quart (30 cm) small roaster.

3 red or orange bell peppers
1 onion, chopped finely
1 teaspoon butter, softened
3 firm tomatoes, skinned and chopped
2 garlic cloves, crushed
2 cups (125 g) fresh white bread crumbs
1 tablespoon fresh chopped flat-leaf parsley
9 pitted ripe olives, chopped
a little olive oil, for drizzling
salt and freshly ground black pepper

1 Cut the peppers in half horizontally through the stem end, leaving the pieces of stem attached, but removing the seeds and any fleshy filaments.

2 Put the onion and butter into a small microwave dish and microwave on full power for 1 to 1½ minutes to soften the onion. (If you do not have a microwave, fry it gently in a small skillet.)

3 Preheat the oven to 375°F/190°C/Gas Mark 5. Mix together the tomatoes, onion, garlic, bread crumbs, parsley, and olives with plenty of seasoning. Spoon this mixture into the pepper shells, packing it down a little because it will shrink while being roasted.

4 Stand the filled peppers in the lightly greased roaster and drizzle a little olive oil over the top of each.

5 Roast in the oven for 45 to 50 minutes until the peppers are tender and slightly charred around the top edges.

This recipe can also be cooked in the base of the 2½-quart (26 cm) buffet casserole, or the 14-inch (36 cm) au gratin dish.

These roasted peppers are also delicious served cold as part of a salad buffet.

The same filling can be used for stuffing zucchini shells or scooped-out eggplant halves.

Finely chop the scooped-out flesh and add it to the stuffing.

CELEBRATION TURKEY WITH CELERY AND APPLE STUFFING

Serves 10–12
Preparation time: 30 minutes
Cooking time: 3 to 4 hours

The stuffing for this turkey recipe is packed with fruits and vegetables, and it slices well to be served with hot or cold turkey. This recipe uses a 6½-quart (40 cm) roaster.

12 to 14 pound (6 to 7 kg) fresh
  turkey
butter, softened, for rubbing on the
  turkey

For the celery and apple stuffing:
½ cup (60 g) bacon, chopped
2 tablespoons (30 g) butter,
  softened
1 medium onion, chopped finely
3 celery stalks, chopped finely
2 medium cooking apples, grated
1 cup (150 g) roughly chopped
  ready-to-eat dried apricots
2 cups (125 g) fresh white bread
  crumbs
2 tablespoons chopped fresh
  parsley
1 tablespoon chopped fresh thyme
1 large egg, beaten
salt and freshly ground black
  pepper

For the gravy:
2 cups (500 ml) turkey stock
1 cup (250 ml) port wine
1 tablespoon cornstarch

1 To make the stuffing, put the bacon into a saucepan over medium heat and cook until the fat begins to run. Add the butter, onion, and celery and continue cooking until the vegetables begin to soften, but not brown. Remove the pan from the heat and leave to cool slightly.

2 Transfer the bacon and vegetables to a large bowl and stir in the apples, apricots, bread crumbs, herbs, egg, and plenty of seasoning. Leave to cool completely.

3 Preheat the oven to 350°F/180°C/Gas Mark 4. Pack the stuffing tightly into the neck cavity of the turkey and secure the neck flap of skin over it with turkey skewers or strong string.

4 Lightly grease the roasting pan. Add the turkey breast side up, brushing the butter over the top, and adding plenty of

seasoning. Cover lightly with a piece of buttered aluminum foil.

5 Transfer the pan to the oven and roast for 3½ to 4 hours, basting with the cooking juices at least once. Remove the foil for the last 30 minutes of roasting to brown and crisp the skin. To check if the turkey is cooked through, pierce the thickest part of the leg with a metal skewer – the juices will run clear when it is cooked.

6 Transfer the turkey to a warm serving platter or carving tray. Cover with foil and a dish towel, and leave to rest for 15 minutes before carving.

7 While the turkey is resting, make the gravy. Pour the fat out of the roasting pan. Place the pan on the stovetop and pour in the stock and port wine. Bring slowly to a boil, stirring to release any residues. Blend the cornstarch with a little cold water and stir this into the hot liquid. Continue simmering and stirring until the gravy thickens. Taste and add seasoning as required. Carve the turkey and serve with a little of the stuffing and gravy.

 Frozen turkey must be very thoroughly thawed before cooking. Plan to leave a bird of this size at least 48 hours in the refrigerator before roasting.
  To guarantee adequate heat penetration to the inside of the turkey, it is best to pack just the neck flap with the stuffing, rather than the body cavity. After cooking, the skin can then be peeled away so the stuffing can be sliced and served with the turkey meat.

 Beaujolais or a light red from the Loire Valley (Chinon or Bourgueil) will make a nice partner. If you prefer a white wine, try a Riesling or a Gewurztraminer.

FRENCH-STYLE ROAST LAMB WITH BEANS AND RED WINE

Serves 8 to 10
Preparation time: 15 minutes
Cooking time: 3 to 3½ hours

This is a very good way to cook a leg of lamb. The slightly steamy atmosphere created by the stock and wine produces very juicy and tender meat. The beans added at the end, along with the vegetables and herbs, make this a very robust and rustic dish. This recipe uses the 6½-quart (40 cm) roaster.

4 to 5 pound (2 to 2½ kg) leg of lamb
2 garlic cloves, cut into quarters
8 sprigs rosemary, broken into small pieces
12 shallots, peeled and left whole
8 large carrots, cut into large chunks
a little vegetable oil, for greasing
1 cup (250 ml) chicken or lamb stock
2 cups (500 ml) full-bodied, dry red wine
1 pound (450 g) canned flageolet or cannellini beans, drained and rinsed
2 teaspoons red-currant jelly
1 tablespoon cornstarch
salt and freshly ground black pepper

1 Preheat the oven to 350°F/180°C/Gas Mark 4. Trim the lamb of any excess pieces of fat. Pierce the flesh several times and push pieces of garlic and rosemary into the holes.

2 Place the lamb in the lightly greased roaster. Brush a little oil over the top and season well.

3 Put all the prepared vegetables around the lamb with any remaining excess pieces of rosemary, the stock, and 1 cup (250 ml) of the wine. Cover the top loosely with a piece of aluminum foil.

4 Transfer to the oven and roast for 1 hour, then reduce the temperature to 325°F/160°C/Gas Mark 3 and continue roasting for about 2 hours longer. The meat should still be a little pink at this stage.

5 Remove the foil and add the beans around the meat. Return the pan, uncovered, to the oven for 30 to 45 minutes longer until the meat is cooked to the degree you prefer.

6 Transfer the lamb to a warm serving platter or carving tray. Cover with foil and a dish towel and leave to rest for 10 to 15 minutes. While the lamb is resting, make the sauce. Remove most of the vegetables using a slotted spoon; keep these hot. Place the pan over a medium heat on the stovetop. Add the remaining wine and bring the liquid to a boil. Stir in the red-currant jelly and cornstarch blended with a little cold water. Simmer, stirring, until the sauce is thick and glossy.

7 Carve the lamb thickly and serve each portion with a few of the vegetables and beans and some sauce spooned over.

A 3 to 3½ pound (1½ kg) leg of lamb can be roasted in the 12-inch (30 cm) roaster.

Potato Dauphinois (on page 73) goes particularly well with this dish.

Red Bordeaux is the classic partner for lamb. Wines from St. Emilion and Pomerol will work beautifully. An American Merlot, particularly from hillside or mountain vineyards, will also go well.

TIRAMISU

Serves 10

Preparation time: 20 minutes

Cooking time: 8 minutes for the ladyfingers

The title of this popular Italian dessert literally means "pick me up". My version is a somewhat simplified recipe of the traditional because I have found, over years of making this, that more and more people have an intolerance to raw or lightly cooked eggs. This recipe does not contain any eggs, but still ends up with the correct, firm consistency that can be cut into squares. It is generously laced with brandy, but rum or Italian Marsala wine can also be used. This recipe uses the 2½-quart (30 cm) small roaster, which has the perfect depth and shape for this dessert.

40 pairs of ladyfingers cookies
1 pound (450 g) mascarpone
   cheese
⅓ cup (75 g) sugar
1 cup (250 ml) heavy cream,
   beaten lightly
⅓ cup (80 ml) brandy
4 cups (1 litre) strong black coffee
2 tablespoons unsweetened
   cocoa powder, sifted

1 Preheat the oven to 350°F/180°C/Gas Mark 4. Spread the cookies out on a cookie sheet and bake in the heated oven for 8 to 10 minutes until firm, crisp, and golden. Set aside to cool thoroughly on a cooling rack.

2 Beat the cheese and sugar together until light and fluffy. Add the cream and brandy, beating these lightly, but not so much that the mixture becomes too stiff: it should have a soft dropping consistency.

3 Pour the coffee into a flat bowl, such as a pie plate. Dip each pair of ladyfingers very quickly into the coffee. Make a single layer in the bottom of the roaster, using half the cookies.

4 Spread half the cheese mixture over, then add the second layer of dipped cookies, and finally the second layer of the cheese. Using a round-bladed knife, make a scrolled line pattern over the cheese mixture. Cover with plastic wrap and chill for 5 to 6 hours.

5 Before serving, sprinkle the cocoa powder liberally over the surface.

Low-fat whipping cream can be used for this recipe.
   Baking the ladyfinger cookies (to make them firmer) can be done the day before making the tiramisu.

When entertaining, this recipe can be made 1 or 2 days in advance to the end of Step 4, then covered tightly and chilled until required. Do not add the cocoa powder until the day it is to be served.

A tawny Port or a malmsey Madeira would be the ideal partner for this dessert.

Honey Cake

Makes 16 slices

Preparation time: 10 minutes

Cooking time: 45 to 50 minutes

This is one of the simplest cakes to make, and is especially good when you need cakes for a crowd – family picnics, school fundraisers, or simply school packed lunches. It can be cut into squares or larger slices, to suit any appetite, and it keeps well in an airtight container. Make this in the 2½-quart (30 cm) roaster.

2 sticks (225 g) butter or
   margarine, softened
1½ cups (225 g) light soft brown
   sugar, unpacked
½ cup (185 g) honey
⅓ cup (80 ml) water
3½ cups (450 g) self-rising flour,
   sifted
¼ teaspoon salt
3 large eggs, beaten
⅓ cup (25 g) slivered almonds

1 Preheat the oven to 325°F/160°C/Gas Mark 3. Line the roaster with parchment baking paper. Put the butter or margarine, brown sugar, honey, and ⅓ cup (80 ml) water into a large saucepan over low heat and melt the ingredients together. Do not boil. Remove the pan from the heat and set aside to cool slightly.

2 Beat the flour, salt, and eggs into the melted ingredients.

3 Pour the thick batter into the pan and scatter the almonds evenly over the top.

4 Bake the cake in the middle of the oven for 45 to 50 minutes until it is golden brown and springy to the touch. Leave the cake to cool in the pan for for 10 to 15 minutes before unmolding and leaving to cool on a cooling rack. Cool completely before cutting and storing.

Always sift flour before it is mixed into hot or warm ingredients to prevent lumps from forming.

Do not open the oven door while baking cake batters with *rising agents in them. If the cake is not fully set in the middle, it can sink from the rush of cold air.*

WOKS & MOROCCAN TAGINES

Today we live in a shrinking world where the accessibility to other cultures and their indigenous foods has never been greater or more enjoyable. The rapid growth in the food supply industry offers us the opportunity to re-create dishes from all corners of the globe and many styles of cooking are now so established as to be commonplace. Ten years ago, who would have thought that stir-frying would have the international status it enjoys today and will probably still have in years to come?

Le Creuset has kept abreast of these developments by producing "speciality shapes" based on very traditional designs. The wok and tagine originate in countries far apart, but their purpose has always been to cook a huge array of foods. When stovetop space or cooking fuel, such as charcoal, was limited in the past, cooks had to be ingenious and learn how to adapt. And adapt they did, but in ways which we should hold in awe. Even the simplest of meals became a small banquet, offering a variety of sweet and savory dishes with which to tempt the family and guests.

The Wok

"Le chi fan meu?" literally means, "Have you eaten yet?" It is often used as a greeting in China, in the same way we would ask, "How are you?" This demonstrates clearly how important food is to most Chinese. The wok found in any Chinese home today is the same shape it has been for centuries. It has, over that time, been the core of a somewhat limited number of cooking vessels, as most Chinese kitchens do not have more than a rice boiler, a layered bamboo steamer, an earthenware casserole and a wok.

Early woks were made from beaten raw cast iron and the rounded shape of the base was designed to nestle snuggly into charcoal. But this shape also had another purpose which has caused Chinese cuisine to become so popular: the very rounded and narrow base of the wok meant that very little oil was required to fry and cook quite large quantities of meats and vegetables and the cast iron was able to transmit heat extremely efficiently. Oil and fuel were both, until more recent years, expensive commodities. So to be able to use only a little of both and still create a delicious meal was obviously a great advantage. Although only the base of the wok actually sat in the coals, the heat transfer through the material meant that the side wall became hot as well and, as foods were added in succession, they could be pushed from the hot area in the base to a warm holding zone on the side wall. This is also a characteristic of the Le Creuset wok today. But Le Creuset has also added some refinements to make it more suitable for modern fuels and uses. Most importantly, it has a flat outer base so no matter which stovetop it is used on, the heat transfer will always be efficient. This flat base has not, however, compromised the inner curved shape, so integral to successful cooking with a wok. Secondly, it is completely covered in porcelain enamel so, apart from washing, it really needs no other preparation or seasoning. The black inner porcelain enamel will change color with use and become covered in a "patina" and as any Chinese cook will tell you, this is just as it should be: the blacker the wok, the better the cooking results will be. The wok also has a lid and two large side-lifting handles for ease of maneuverability. The lid transforms the wok into quite the most amazing multi-function cooking vessel which can be used for braising, boiling, steaming and frying. As I said earlier, when space and cooking facilities are limited, ingenuity and adaptability prevail.

But open stir-frying is probably what most people purchase a wok for, as it does it so well and so much better than other flatter shaped utensils. Apart from the speed with which a stir-fry dish can, and should, be produced, the health benefits it provides are exceptional. Stir-fries are very low in fat, use less red meat and prefer the use of brightly colored vegetables with a little chicken or fish. The Chinese diet is based on balance and uses harmful foods only in moderation. The Chinese enjoy using fresh, local produce which is available in the market that day and so their menus are defined by the seasons. The emphasis on harmony, the care they take with their food and their healthy and fascinating cooking methods undoubtedly contribute to their excellent health record.

Wok General Tips

- Stir-frying is a very quick method of cooking, therefore it is vital to have all the ingredients prepared before cooking begins.
- Although stir-frying is quick, the wok should not be used over a high heat. Medium and low heats will provide ample heat for all stir-fry and deep-fat frying.
- Traditionally, peanut oil is used for most Chinese cookery. It is light and gives excellent results without transferring any additional flavor to the food. Sesame, walnut and other flavored oils can be used in small quantities to impart their own special flavor, but are best used mixed with another oil to avoid overpowering the food they are cooking. Olive oil, butter, margarine or white fats are not ideal. They can burn too easily and have too strong a flavor.
- The lid is sometimes used to cover and lightly steam ingredients at the end of stir-frying (see the recipe for Peppered Pork on page 92). This is very traditional and helps soften very crisp vegetables, while retaining their "bite" or color. It is particularly useful for those who find very crisp vegetables a little too indigestible.
- When stir-frying for a crowd, the time to cook can be accelerated by pre-blanching (for just 1 minute) really crisp vegetables, such as carrots and green beans. This will mean they take less time to cook in the wok.
- When deep-fat frying for tempura recipes, the oil level must be kept low and 2 cups (500 ml) is the advised maximum for the larger wok. In this way, as foods are added, the hot oil will not rise up over the rim of the wok.
- A tempura draining rack is a useful accessory to rest on the rim of the wok. It allows fried foods to drain, while remaining crisp and hot.
- An enclosed 10-inch (25 cm) bamboo steamer can be used inside the larger 4¼-quart (36 cm) wok. An 8" bamboo steamer can be used in the 2¼-quart wok.

There are two sizes of Le Creuset wok. The larger is a 4¼-quart (36 cm) wok and will cook for six to eight people. The smaller 2¼-quart (28 cm) wok is ideal for two people.

The Moroccan Tagine

The tagine originates in North Africa where a number of different cultural influences have combined to create something unique. The people who live here have their roots in a variety of ancient civilizations that invaded, traded and visited these shores as they crossed continents. A tagine is as significant to the cooking of North African food as the wok is to Chinese cuisine and its design is not by accident, but by necessity. Fuel and water are two precious elements in this region and both have to be used frugally. Charcoal fires are almost the only form of "cooking stoves" they have and the wide shallow base of the tagine can be pushed down among the coals to take full advantage of their heat. The tall conical lid was not designed on a whim. It allows the smallest amount of water to be used to moisten the ingredients in the base and the steam it produces, on hitting the tall cool conical side, re-condenses to trickle back down over the gently simmering food. Just a few tablespoons added at the beginning of a recipe will produce sufficient liquid to serve a number of people when the tagine dish is cooked.

The Le Creuset tagine has been modelled very closely on the traditional design. However, as terracotta is not suitable to use directly on our stovetops, the base has been re-created in cast iron. This allows for the very slow and even heat transfer which a tagine needs to provide for the food. The conical lid, which is made from glazed earthenware, allows just the same pattern of re-condensation of the steam, but the glazed finish makes it less porous and therefore cleaner and easier to use.

The tagine can be used for a wide variety of meat, vegetable and fruit dishes. Fruit cooked with meat and vegetables are commonplace and provide a natural sweetness to many dishes. The timing for cooking in the tagine is intended to be slow, and hours of cooking, rather than minutes, should be expected. However, on modern stovetops the cooking of such dishes will inevitably be a little faster than when the same dish is cooked over coals so if in a traditional recipe it is left for 8 to 10 hours, it will probably be cooked as well in 4 to 6 hours in the Le Creuset tagine. The Moroccan Tagine comes in just one size and will cook recipes to serve 4 to 6 people.

General Tips

- A tagine is intended for stovetop use only, where its heating and cooking qualities are used to the full. If placed in the oven, while not causing permanent damage, the lid and base will become too hot and the lid, in particular, will simply evaporate the cooking liquid instead of condensing it.
- The cast iron base can be used on its own and makes a useful baking, roasting and serving dish.
- On the stovetop the cast iron base can be used for pre-browning meats, poultry and vegetables before the slow-cooking process begins. Like all other pieces of Le Creuset cast iron, pre-browning should be done on medium and low heats only.
- The adjustment to a very low setting for cooking is important and there should be barely a ripple of movement in the food as it cooks. If, due to the design of your stovetop this "very

low" heat is not really achievable don't be concerned, cooking at a slightly faster pace will give just as good a result. But do then be aware that more steam will be produced and this can sometimes seep up around the rim between the base and the lid.

- Although the very top of the conical lid will remain relatively cool, the base of it will not, and when removing the lid to check the contents a cloth or oven mitts should be used to lift and support this rim edge, holding the top of the lid with the other hand.
- Both the base and lid can be washed in hot, soapy water. The lid may not appear to need washing but the unglazed rim may have absorbed some grease which should be washed off. To ensure excess moisture is not absorbed into the lid, do not soak it in water. Resting it on its side for a short while after washing and drying will allow the earthenware to dry out before storage.

PEPPERED PORK STIR-FRY

Serves 4

Preparation time: 15 minutes

Cooking time: 6 to 7 minutes

Marinating the pork in the cornstarch and other spicy ingredients produces the very glossy and pungent flavor that many recipes from the Szechuan region of China are known for. The marinating time can be as little as half an hour, but leave the meat longer if you have time. This recipe uses the 4¼-quart (36 cm) wok.

1 pound (450 g) pork tenderloin, cut into finger-size pieces

For the marinade:

2 teaspoons cornstarch

2 tablespoons dark soy sauce

2 tablespoons saké or dry sherry

2 tablespoons peanut oil

1 garlic clove, crushed

2 small red chilies, chopped finely

1 teaspoon sugar

a little freshly ground black pepper

For the stir-fry:

2 tablespoons peanut oil

6 scallions, white parts only, sliced thinly

½ red, ½ yellow, and ½ orange bell pepper, seeded and cut into thin strips

4½ ounces (125 g) snow peas

1 tablespoon dark soy sauce

½ teaspoon sesame oil

To serve:

fried rice or boiled plain rice or noodles

1 To make the marinade, mix all the marinade ingredients together in a Le Creuset gratin dish. Add the pork and turn in the marinade so that it is evenly coated. Cover and leave to stand for 30 minutes to 1 hour in the refrigerator. Drain the pork well and pat it dry with paper towels before stir-frying.

2 Heat 1 tablespoon of the oil in the wok over medium heat on the stovetop. Add the scallions and stir-fry, until they are just beginning to soften. Push these up onto the side wall of the wok. Add the bell peppers and snow peas and stir-fry for 1 to 2 minutes, pushing these up onto the side

wall as well. Add the remaining oil to the wok, and when it is hot, add the pork and stir-fry for 2 to 3 minutes until it is tender.

3 When the pork is cooked, push all the vegetables back into the middle of the wok. Add the soy sauce, sesame oil, 1 tablespoon of water, and a little ground black pepper. Stir together.

Taste before adding any salt because the soy sauce will add its own saltiness and this might be sufficient. Serve immediately with fried rice or boiled plain rice or noodles.

 Half the quantity of this recipe can be stir-fried in the smaller 2¼-quart (28 cm) mini wok.

 Have all the ingredients prepared before stir-frying begins.

This recipe can also be made with sliced, skinned chicken breasts.

BRAISED ORANGE DUCK

Serves 6

Preparation time: 10 minutes + 15 minutes boiling

Cooking time: 3 to 3½ hours

Chinese braising, like stir-frying, is an excellent way to cook a "meal in a wok". The long, slow cooking of the duck on a bed of vegetables and orange zest results in a very tender dish, full of intense flavors. The parboiling of the duck removes a considerable amount of its fat and helps to make the meat very tender. The 4¼-quart (36 cm) wok is used for this recipe.

6 duck legs
2 tablespoons peanut oil
6 scallions, chopped roughly
6 shallots, quartered
3 carrots, cut into finger-size
    pieces
pared zest of 2 large oranges
2 tablespoons dark soy sauce
4 tablespoons fresh orange juice
1 teaspoon Chinese five-spice
    powder
4 stars of star anise
freshly ground black pepper
boiled rice, to serve

1 Trim the duck of excess flaps of skin or fat, or remove the skin if preferred. Put all the duck pieces into the wok, cover with boiling water, and bring to a boil. Reduce the heat, cover with the wok lid, and simmer gently for 15 minutes. Remove the duck and discard the cooking liquid. Dry the duck on paper towels.

2 Rinse and dry the wok. Heat the oil in the wok over a medium heat. Add the duck, a few pieces at a time, and brown evenly on both sides. Remove the duck with a slotted spoon, draining well.

3 When all the duck is browned, add the vegetables to the hot oil and stir-fry for 2 to 3 minutes until they begin to soften and color.

4 Return the duck pieces to the wok on top of the vegetables. Add the orange zest, all of the remaining ingredients, and 4 tablespoons of water, pushing the star anise and orange zest down between the duck pieces.

5 Cover the wok and cook over very low heat on the stovetop for 3 to 3½ hours until the duck is very tender and the vegetables are almost to a purée. Remove the orange zest and star anise pieces before serving. Serve with boiled rice.

 This recipe can also be cooked in the 3½-quart (30 cm) buffet casserole or the 11-inch (28 cm) sauté pan with a lid.

 Chicken leg quarters can also be used in this recipe. They do not require boiling, and only need 2 to 2½ hours cooking time.

SHRIMP AND VEGETABLE TEMPURA WITH SWEET-AND-SOUR SAUCE

Serves 6 as an appetizer

Preparation time: 25 minutes + 10 minutes for the sauce

Cooking time: 15 minutes

It is very important that the wok is not overfilled with the frying oil, because as the ingredients are added, the level rises and any excess water on them can cause spitting. Do not use more than 2 cups (500 ml) oil. This tempura batter uses carbonated water, which gives a much lighter result than either milk or water. This recipe uses the 4¼-quart (36 cm) wok.

2 cups (225 g) all-purpose flour
½ teaspoon salt
1 teaspoon ground hot chili powder
2 large eggs, beaten
1½ cups (375 ml) carbonated water
salad garnish

For the shrimp and vegetables:
2¼ pounds (1 kg) shelled, raw jumbo shrimp
3 cups (500 g) broccoli, broken into small florets
4 cups (500 g) zucchini, cut into 2-inch (5 cm) finger-size pieces
2 tablespoons all-purpose flour

For the sweet-and-sour sauce:
2 tablespoons peanut oil
2 shallots, chopped finely
1 garlic clove, chopped finely
3 tablespoons dark soy sauce
2 tablespoons tomato paste
3 tablespoons honey
½ cup (125 ml) fresh orange juice
1½ teaspoons cornstarch
freshly ground black pepper

1   To make the tempura batter, put the flour, salt, and chili powder into a bowl. Add the eggs and half the carbonated water and beat until smooth. Stir in the remaining carbonated water, then set aside to stand for 1 hour.

2   To make the sauce, heat the oil in a small saucepan over medium heat. Add the shallots and garlic and fry gently until the shallots are soft. Stir in all of the remaining ingredients, except the cornstarch, and add 4 tablespoons of water.

3   Simmer for 10 minutes. Blend the cornstarch with a little water, and stir into the sauce; continue simmering and stirring until the sauce is thick. Cook for 1 minute, then remove from the heat and add seasoning to taste.

4   Heat the oil in the wok to 350°F (180°C), or until a piece of bread dropped into the oil rises to the surface and is golden brown in 30 seconds.

5   Quickly dip the shrimp into the flour and then into the batter, shaking off any excess. Drop them into the hot oil with a few pieces of the vegetables dipped in the batter.

6   Fry the shrimp and vegetables for 2 to 3 minutes until the batter is puffed up and pale golden brown: the shrimp must be thoroughly cooked, but the vegetables should still have a little "bite" to them. Drain on a tempura rack resting on the wok rim to keep hot while frying the remaining ingredients.

7   Reheat the sauce and divide between three small dishes so two guests can share a dish. Serve the mixed tempura with the dipping sauce and a salad garnish.

   For extra safety when deep-frying, use an oil thermometer to check the temperature. This will also guarantee crisp results.

Discard the frying oil after use because it will contain pieces of batter and will be flavored from the shrimp.

FISH TAGINE WITH COUSCOUS

Serves 4

Preparation time: 10 minutes + marinating

Cooking time: 1¼ to 1½ hours

Not all tagine recipes have to cook for hours, and here the spicy vegetable sauce is only cooked for about an hour before the fish is added. If it is more convenient, the sauce can be made ahead, to be reheated with whatever fresh fish you are serving. It is delicious served with couscous, or alternatively, with plain boiled rice.

2¼ pounds (1 kg) firm white fish such as cod, monkfish, or halibut

For the marinade:

1 small red chili, seeded and chopped finely
2 garlic cloves, crushed
1 teaspoon ground coriander
1 teaspoon ground cumin
1 teaspoon turmeric
2 tablespoons olive oil
finely grated zest of 1 lemon
4 tablespoons lemon juice

For the sauce:

2 tablespoons olive oil
1 small onion, chopped coarsely
4⅓ cups (350 g) eggplant cut into ½-inch (1 cm) cubes

1 potato, peeled and cut into ½-inch (1 cm) cubes
1 pound (450 g) canned plum tomatoes, chopped with their juice
1 teaspoon tomato paste
2 tablespoons fresh chopped cilantro
⅓ cup (60 g) pitted green olives
salt and freshly ground black pepper

For the couscous, to serve:

2 cups (350 g) couscous
2 cups (500 ml) boiling water or chicken stock
2 teaspoons olive oil

1 Mix together all the marinade ingredients in a Le Creuset gratin dish or a non-metallic bowl. Cut the fish into large chunks and add it to the marinade, gently turning it so that it is evenly coated. Cover and leave to marinate in the refrigerator for 1 to 2 hours.

2 Heat the oil for the sauce in the tagine base over medium heat on the stovetop. Add the onion, eggplant, and potatoes and fry until they are just beginning to color and become soft.

3 Add the tomatoes and their juice with the tomato paste. Add

1 tablespoon of the cilantro, and some seasoning. Cover with the tagine lid and cook over very low heat for 1 to 1¼ hours until the vegetables are tender.

4 To prepare the couscous, put it into a large bowl, pour the boiling water or stock over, cover with a plate, and leave to stand for 10 minutes. Add the olive oil and stir to separate the grains.

5 Transfer the couscous to a fine-mesh strainer or colander lined with a piece of cheesecloth. Place over a saucepan or French oven filled with hot water, cover, and steam for 10 to 15 minutes to heat through. Season with a little salt and pepper before serving.

6 While the couscous is cooking, add the fish to the sauce, together with any remaining marinade and the olives. Re-cover the tagine and cook for 10 to 15 minutes longer until the fish is cooked.

7 Sprinkle with the remaining cilantro and serve with the steamed couscous.

 This recipe can also be made in the 2½-quart (26 cm) buffet casserole.

 To make ahead, complete the recipe to the end of Step 3, then cool completely, cover, and chill until it is time to reheat. Bring the sauce to a simmer, add the fresh fish and proceed from Step 4.

 A big, fruit-driven California Zinfandel can handle the spice of this dish quite well. If you use a great deal of chili, a cold lager beer may be the best option.

STEAMED SEA BASS WITH NOODLES

Serves 2
Preparation time: 10 minutes
Cooking time: 15 minutes

This is a typically Eastern way to cook fish. It results in the fish being plump and moist, and gently perfumed with the flavors of lemon grass and ginger. This recipe is best cooked in the 4¼-quart (36 cm) wok, because it has enough room for a steaming rack to hold the fish above the gently simmering liquid.

two 1 pound (450 g) small sea
    bass, cleaned
1-inch (2.5 cm) piece fresh ginger,
    peeled and sliced very thinly
2 tablespoons chopped fresh
    flat-leaf parsley
3 pieces lemon grass
2 teaspoons light soy sauce
4½ ounces (125 g) dried fine egg
    noodles

1 Cut off the fins, tail, and head of the fish, if preferred. Cut two deep slashes into both sides of the fish and push a few pieces of the ginger and a little of the parsley into the slashes. Cut the lemon grass pieces in half lengthways and put a small piece inside the cavity of each fish.

2 Put 2 cups (500 ml) of water and a piece of lemon grass into the wok over a medium heat on the stovetop. Bring to a boil, then reduce to a gentle simmer. Position a steaming rack in the wok.

3 Place the fish on the rack and scatter over the remaining pieces of lemon grass and sprinkle with 1 teaspoon of the soy sauce. Cover and steam for 8 to 10 minutes.

4 Uncover the wok and carefully lift up the rack holding the fish. Add the dried noodles to the liquid with the remaining chopped parsley. Return the rack and fish to the wok, re-cover and cook for 3 to 4 minutes longer.

5 Remove the fish from the wok and discard the lemon grass. Drain the noodles, discarding the lemon grass. Serve the fish on top of the noodles with the remaining soy sauce sprinkled over the top.

Light soy sauce is more salty than dark, so do not add salt to the recipe until after you have tasted it.

Other small whole fish, such as trout or small sea salmon, can also be used in this recipe.

A Pinot Gris or Muscat from the Alsace region of France are the top choices for this dish. Both will work well with the ginger and lemon grass.

LAMB SHANKS WITH OKRA

Serves 4
Preparation time: 20 minutes
Cooking time: 3½ to 4 hours

This recipe is very typical of the North African-style of tagine cooking, using very little liquid to moisten the ingredients at the beginning, allowing the natural meat and vegetable juices to be released as the dish cooks slowly. Lamb shanks are sold in supermarkets, but any lean lamb cut into large chunks could be used instead.

2 tablespoons olive oil
1 large red onion, sliced thinly
3 small red chilies, seeded and
  chopped
2 garlic cloves, chopped
4 lamb shanks, trimmed of fat and
  gristle
2 teaspoons ground cumin
2 teaspoons ground coriander
1 teaspoon ground turmeric
1 pound (450 g) canned plum
  tomatoes, chopped with their
  juice
¼ teaspoon salt
a pinch of freshly ground black
  pepper
4½ ounces (125 g) fresh okra
1 tablespoon chopped fresh
  flat-leaf parsley, to garnish
plain steamed couscous, to serve

1. Heat the oil in the tagine base over medium heat on the stovetop. Add the onion and fry until it begins to soften and color. Add the chilies and garlic and fry for 1 minute longer. Remove with a slotted spoon, draining well.

2. Add the lamb shanks, two at a time, and brown evenly. Remove each as it becomes brown.

3. Return the onion to the tagine, stir in the spices, and cook slowly for 1 minute, stirring continuously. Add the tomatoes and their juice.

4. Lay the lamb shanks on top, in two layers if necessary. Spoon some of the sauce over them and season well with the salt and pepper.

5. Cover with the tagine lid and simmer over very low heat for 3 to 3½ hours until the lamb shanks are tender, rearranging them after half the time so the ones on the top go to the bottom.

6. When the lamb is tender, push the okra in around the meat

and cook for 30 to 40 minutes longer. Before serving, sprinkle the top with the chopped parsley. Serve with plain steamed couscous (see page 95, Step 4).

This recipe can also be cooked in the 3½-quart (30 cm) buffet casserole or a large round or oval French oven.

Do not touch your face, particularly your eyes, after handling and cutting chilies, because they contain a powerful irritant. Wash your hands, the board and knife thoroughly.

MOROCCAN CHICKEN TAGINE

Serves 4

**Preparation time: 30 minutes
+ 6 hours marinating**

Cooking time: 3 hours

Combining fruit with meat, poultry, or fish is typical of North African cuisine, and with a spicy marinade, the overall flavor is not too sweet. As with many tagine or casserole dishes, the flavors do improve when made a day ahead. If you cook this recipe ahead, stop after Step 6 and then reheat thoroughly from Step 7 and the sauce will become syrupy.

2¼ pounds (1 kg) chicken thighs, skinned

1 tablespoon olive oil

1 large onion, sliced thinly

2 tablespoons light brown sugar

½ cup (125 ml) dry white wine

finely grated zest of 1 large orange

¾ cup (125 g) ready-to-eat dried apricots, cut into quarters

1 tablespoon chopped fresh cilantro, to garnish

For the marinade:

2 teaspoons ground cumin

1 teaspoon ground coriander

½ teaspoon coarsely ground black pepper

½ teaspoon salt

3 garlic cloves, crushed

1 small red chili, seeded and chopped finely

½ cup (125 ml) orange juice

3 tablespoons olive oil

To serve:

plain steamed couscous or boiled plain long-grain rice

1 To make the marinade, mix all the marinade ingredients in a large flat dish such as a Le Creuset gratin dish. Add the chicken thighs and turn them in the marinade so they are well coated. Cover and marinate in the refrigerator for at least 6 hours, or overnight.

2 Heat the oil in the tagine base over medium heat on the stovetop. Add the onion and fry gently until it is just beginning to brown; remove from the pan.

3 Drain the chicken, discarding the marinade, and pat dry with paper towels. Add the chicken pieces to the tagine and fry until they are evenly brown.

4 Return the onion to the tagine with the sugar, wine, and orange zest. Stir well and add a little more salt and pepper.

5 Cover with the tagine lid and simmer over very low heat for 1½ hours.

6 Add the apricots, re-cover, and continue simmering for 1½ hours until the chicken is cooked through and tender.

7 When the chicken is cooked, remove the lid and boil the sauce for a few minutes until it becomes syrupy. Sprinkle liberally with the chopped cilantro and serve with plain steamed couscous (see page 95, Step 4), or boiled, plain long-grain rice.

 This recipe can also be made in the 2½-quart (26 cm) buffet casserole.

 This recipe can also be made with diced leg of lamb, in which case allow another hour for cooking.

 Since this dish is both spicy and sweet, it is well suited to a slightly sweet German Riesling or Gewurztraminer. Try a Spatlese level of sweetness for best results.

FONDUES

The cheese fondue called "Fondue Neuchâtel" is the national dish of Switzerland and this convivial style of eating has been enjoyed for several hundreds of years on the Alpine slopes of that country.

The fondue evolved because during cold winters the small villages were cut off from the towns by snow-covered mountains, and consequently fresh food became scarce. The villagers had to rely on locally-made produce, which included cheeses, bread and wine. As the winter months wore on, so the huge wheels of cheese they produced in the summer months became drier and more unpalatable. From the need to use up this valuable food source, the fondue as we know it today was born. "Fondue" derives from the French verb "fondre" meaning "to melt, or blend". The cheese was broken up and melted in an earthenware pot called a "caquelon" and originally would have been heated over the gentle embers of an open fire.

Today with a cast iron "caquelon" pan, the cheese, or other ingredients, can be melted on any stovetop (or even a gentle barbecue) and then transferred to the convenient table-stand and burner for serving. The first cast iron fondue set, comprising the fondue pot and table-stand with burner, was launched by Le Creuset in 1962. Immediately the benefits of using cast iron for the fondue pot were recognized since, once hot, it could be placed over the table burner and left there; the cook did not have to return it to the kitchen to reheat, which is necessary with fondue pots made of other materials.

The traditional Swiss fondue recipe uses Gruyère or Emmental cheese. These melt well and give a distinctive flavor, but many other cheeses from around the world make equally good fondues. Sharp Cheddar or Monterey Jack can also be used, and for those who are watching the calories, low-fat cheeses will work well too.

Sharing the fun of a fondue evening with friends can lead to forfeits being paid. If, while swirling a piece of bread in a cheese fondue, a lady loses it in the mixture, she has to kiss every gentleman present and if a gentleman does the same, his forfeit is to produce another bottle of wine or glass of kirsch for the host or hostess. If either party makes the same mistake again, *they* have to host the next fondue party!

The choice of drinks at a fondue party is debatable. It is customary not to drink during a fondue, but a glass of "Kirsch" or "Cherry brandy" taken half-way through the proceedings is known as a "coup de mileau". Cold drinks when combined with the warm cheese were thought to cause indigestion, hence the tradition to drink unsweetened warm tea, a glass of schnapps, fruit juices or the same wine used in the fondue itself, such as Hock or Reisling, but at room temperature, not chilled.

During the time it takes for a fondue to be eaten, a delicacy often forms in the bottom of the pot. This brown crust is traditionally flambéed in kirsch before the host prises it away from the base to share with their guests. This process is known as the "religieuse", a symbolic sharing with friends.

Today, fondue flavors are extended to include making sweet recipes as well as savory. The smaller La Saucière is traditionally used for rich chocolate fondues, but can also be used to create an interesting appetizer for a dinner party. Served with fresh crisp vegetables and savory breads, it makes a colorful and eye-catching centerpiece for a dinner party or buffet table.

Sweet fondues also make quick and easy desserts for summer al fresco or barbecue eating. If you are catering for a crowd, two fondue pots full of the Jamaican Calypso Fondue on page 107 will go a long way.

Fondue parties are fun and informal, which sits well with today's more relaxed style of entertaining. They also offer a simple way for the family to meet around the table at weekends.

General Tips

Cheese Fondues

- Use a well-flavored cheese, diced or grated, as it melts more quickly and evenly.
- Use a dry white wine or cider. If in doubt about its dryness, add a teaspoon of lemon juice (which also helps to melt the cheese).
- Make sure the "liquid" is hot before adding the cheese.
- Add the cheese gradually, not all together, and melt each addition before adding more.
- Do not boil the cheese while melting; it will become stringy.
- If the cheese forms a lump, it has been added too quickly. Raise the heat a little and beat well until it breaks down.
- To rescue a curdled fondue, add a little more lemon juice, or stir in a little blended cornstarch.
- If a cheese fondue becomes too thick, add a drop of warmed wine, or a pinch of baking soda. If it is too thin add a little more blended cornstarch.
- Allow half a baguette, or 6 to 8 ounces (175 to 225 g) of bread for each person, leaving a piece of crust on each cut-up piece so that the fondue fork anchors it more securely. Day-old bread is best because fresh and crumbly bread will break up in the mixture.

Stock Fondues for Meat and Fish

- Stock fondues are often called fondue "Chinoise". Meat, poultry and fish can be cooked in stock alone, or in a mixture of stock and sherry. Flavorings such as bay leaves, fresh herbs, garlic, chili or onion will flavor the stock and leftovers can be made into a flavorsome soup by adding some noodles and diced vegetables. The maximum filling level for a stock fondue is two-thirds full.

Oil Fondues for Meat and Fish

- Good quality meat, poultry, fish and vegetables can be cooked in an oil fondue.
- The maximum filling level for an oil fondue is one-third full and this should never be exceeded.

As foods are added to the hot oil it will bubble up and, if the pot is over-full, the oil will spill over the top rim.

- Use good quality peanut or vegetable oil and use the oil only once for a fondue. The oil will collect debris during the cooking period and this will flavor the oil, so it should be discarded.
- Olive oil has a lower smoking point than vegetable oils. It is excellent for flavor, so a little could be mixed into the main oil, but do not use olive oil on its own for cooking.
- The oil is initially heated on the stovetop. It must *never* be left unattended here, or when on the burner stand. Use a thermometer to accurately check the temperature and move the pan very carefully using oven mitts at all times.
- Flavorings such as herbs, garlic and chilies can be used to enhance the flavor of the oil.
- Dry raw meat, poultry and fish on paper towels before putting onto plates for cooking. Any moisture going into the oil will reduce the temperature, cause excessive spitting, and will eventually weaken the oil so that it steams the food rather than quickly searing or frying it.
- Allow approximately 8 ounces (225 g) of meat or fish per person. Anchor the food well on the fondue fork so that it will not drop into the oil.
- Do not try to cook too much raw food at one time. It will reduce the oil temperature so that it will require re-heating on the stovetop. (The burner alone may not be sufficient to regain the required temperature.)
- Never eat straight from the fondue fork, as the food will be very hot! Transfer the food to a clean serving plate, allow to cool a little and eat with a separate fork. Do not put cooked meat back onto the plate where uncooked meat has been.

Dessert Fondues

- *Never* boil a fondue recipe unless stated in the recipe.
- If you want to make chocolate fondues but do not own a smaller Saucière fondue, use a larger one, which works just as well, but remember to keep the burner flame very low.
- Dessert fondues are usually served just warm, so dipped foods *can* be eaten straight from the fondue fork.

How to Use a Fondue

Each fondue pan and stand has its own care and use instruction leaflet with guidance on how to light the burner and so on. Do read this before you begin as each may be slightly different.

- Always supervise children when the fondue set is in use.
- Always place the fondue stand and burner on a heatproof mat or tray.
- Never refill the lamp while it is very hot or alight.

TRADITIONAL CHEESE FONDUE (FONDUE NEUCHÂTEL)

Serves 6 to 8
Preparation time: 10 minutes
Cooking time: 10 to 15 minutes

This fondue can be made with either of the traditional Swiss cheeses, Gruyère or Emmental, as both produce the authentic consistency. Cubes of day-old bread, with a little crust left on them, are the best for dipping as they anchor well on the fondue forks. Allow half a baguette or 6 to 8 ounces (175 to 225 g) of bread per person. Crisp vegetables such as celery or carrots also go well with this fondue. This recipe is made in the 1½-quart Traditional fondue.

1 garlic clove, halved
1½ cups (375 ml) dry white wine
4 cups (500 g) coarsely grated
    Gruyère cheese
3 teaspoons cornstarch
2 tablespoons kirsch or vodka
a pinch of ground nutmeg
a little freshly ground black pepper

1   Rub the inside of the fondue pan with the cut side of the garlic; this imparts a slight flavor to the pot that will not overpower the flavors of the cheese. Discard the garlic.

2   Pour the wine into the pan and bring to a boil over a medium heat on the stovetop. Reduce the heat to low and gradually add the grated cheese; a small handful at a time is a good measure. Stir thoroughly to melt each handful before adding more. If too much cheese is added at once, it can become stringy or stick together in an unmanageable lump, making it difficult to melt and form the smooth consistency you require.

3   Blend the cornstarch with the kirsch or vodka and stir into the fondue. Continue cooking and stirring until the mixture is thick and creamy. Stir in the nutmeg. Add pepper to taste.

4   Transfer the fondue pot to the stand with the lit spirit burner. Adjust the flame to a lower heat by moving the lever on the burner to close off some of the holes. A low heat will be sufficient to keep the cheese smooth and warm without sticking.

Monterey Jack cheese can also be used for this fondue. If kirsch or vodka are not available, or are not liked, use a little more white wine to blend with the cornstarch.

CREAMY MUSHROOM FONDUE

Serves 6

Preparation time: 10 minutes

Cooking time: 20 minutes

For a party, stand the fondue set on a large serving dish and surround it with colorful raw vegetables, crackers, savory biscuits or breads, then use it as part of a buffet table.

½ stick (60 g) butter
1 onion, chopped finely
2 garlic cloves, chopped finely
12 ounces (350 g) button
  mushrooms, chopped roughly
3 tablespoons all-purpose flour
2 cups (500 ml) milk
1 cup (125 g) coarsely grated
  Gruyère cheese
4 tablespoons heavy cream
4 tablespoons dry sherry
2 tablespoons chopped fresh
  parsley
salt and freshly ground black
  pepper

For dipping:

cubes of French bread
small cooked sausages
raw vegetables, such as carrot
  and celery sticks

1 Melt the butter in the fondue pot over medium heat on the stovetop. Add the onion, garlic, and mushrooms and cook for 10 minutes until soft, but not colored; lower the heat if necessary.

2 Sprinkle in the flour and continue cooking slowly for 1 minute longer, stirring. Remove the pot from the heat and gradually stir in the milk until smooth. Return the pot to the heat and bring to a boil, stirring constantly until the sauce thickens.

3 Remove the pot from the heat and stir in the cheese a little at a time, stirring until it melts, then add the cream, sherry and parsley, with salt and pepper to taste.

4 Transfer the fondue pot to the stand with the lit spirit burner to keep warm, stirring occasionally.

 Half the quantity of this recipe can be made in the smaller La Saucière fondue.

 Fresh wild mushrooms can also be used in this recipe. Replace 4 ounces (125 g) of the button mushrooms with wild mushrooms.

INDIAN-STYLE FONDUE WITH CRUDITÉS

Serves 6
Preparation time: 10 minutes
Cooking time: 15 minutes

A curry-flavored cheese fondue might sound an unlikely combination, but it really is delicious and can be used as an appetizer to an Indian meal. Serve it very simply with bread, or a selection of crudités (see below).

1 garlic clove, halved
1 tablespoon (15 g) butter
1 small onion, chopped finely
2 teaspoons medium-hot curry
   paste
1 cup (250 ml) dry white wine
2 teaspoons lemon juice
3 cups (375 g) coarsely grated
   Gruyère cheese
1 tablespoon dry sherry
2 teaspoons cornstarch
3 tablespoons plain low-fat yogurt

For dipping:
a selection of bread cubes, such
   as naan bread, mixed grain
   breads or foccacia
celery sticks, carrot sticks,
   cauliflower florets and cooked
   potato cubes

1 Rub the inside of the fondue pan with the cut pieces of garlic; discard the garlic.

2 Melt the butter in the fondue pot over medium heat on the stovetop. Add the onion and fry slowly for 4 to 5 minutes until soft and pale golden brown. Stir in the curry paste and cook for 1 minute longer.

3 Pour in the wine and lemon juice and heat slowly until bubbling. Reduce the heat and stir in the cheese little by little, stirring after each addition to make sure it melts before you add more.

4 Blend the sherry and cornstarch together, then stir them into the cheese fondue and continue cooking for 2 to 3 minutes until the mixture thickens.

5 Transfer the fondue pot to the lit spirit burner to keep warm. Just before serving, swirl in the yogurt.

CRAB FONDUE

Serves 6

Preparation time: 10 minutes

Cooking time: 15 minutes

Although white crabmeat undoubtedly gives the best appearance, you can also use a combination of white and dark meats to enjoy a stronger flavor.

½ stick (60 g) butter

4 scallions, chopped finely

1 cup (250 ml) milk

2 cups (225 g) grated Gruyère cheese

½ cup (125 g) cream cheese, flavored with chives

1 tablespoon cornstarch

3 tablespoons dry sherry

8 ounces (225 g) fresh crabmeat, flaked

a pinch of ground mace

a pinch of ground nutmeg

salt and freshly ground black pepper

For dipping:

wholewheat or mixed-grain bread cubes

cooked baby corn cobs or cooked potato cubes

raw vegetables such as broccoli florets and strips of bell pepper

1 Melt the butter in the fondue pot over medium heat on the stovetop. Add the scallions and cook for 1 minute to soften them slightly.

2 Pour in the milk and bring it to a boil.

3 Reduce the heat to low and add the cheese a little at a time, stirring after each addition to make sure it melts before you add more.

4 Stir in the cream cheese and continue stirring until it melts.

5 In a small bowl, blend the cornstarch with the sherry. Stir this into the fondue pot and continue simmering and stirring until the cornstarch thickens the mixture and is cooked through.

6 Stir in the crabmeat, mace, and nutmeg with the salt and pepper to taste.

7 Transfer the pot to the fondue stand with the lit spirit burner, stirring occasionally to keep the mixture smooth.

 Canned crab meat can also be used when fresh crab meat is not available. Drain the canned meat well.

 Try a California Sauvignon Blanc or a Pouilly Fumé or Sancerre from the Loire Valley with the crab. A dry Alsace Pinot Gris or Gewurtztraminer will also work well since Gruyère is used in the dish.

Jamaican Calypso Fondue

Serves 6

Preparation time: 5 minutes

Cooking time: 10 minutes

Use fresh pineapple when it is available. The flesh can be scooped out, puréed, and used in place of canned. The pineapple shells make superb "baskets" for serving the dipping ingredients in.

2 pounds (900 g) canned crushed
  pineapple
4 tablespoons sugar
1 cup (250 ml) low-fat whipping
  cream
2 tablespoons cornstarch
2 tablespoons lemon juice
4 tablespoons Malibu or white rum

For dipping:
ginger and chocolate cookies
cake cubes
macaroons
bite-size pieces of fresh coconut

1 Place the pineapple and its juice, the sugar, and the cream in the fondue pot over medium heat on the stovetop, stirring occasionally.

2 Blend the cornstarch with the lemon juice and Malibu or white rum. Add to the fondue, stirring constantly until the mixture thickens slightly.

3 Transfer the fondue pot to the stand with the lit spirit burner to keep warm.

If using fresh pineapple, choose two medium-size ones that are fairly ripe, so that the flesh will be easy to scoop out.

This makes an ideal recipe for "al fresco" dining alongside the barbecue.

BITTER CHOCOLATE AND ORANGE FONDUE

Serves 6
Preparation time: 5 minutes
Cooking time: 10 minutes

If you have any choc-o-holics in your family, or among friends, this fondue is a must! Fresh plump strawberries or figs go particularly well and will help to ease concerns about any calories in this recipe. This fondue is made in the small La Saucière or chocolate fondue which uses a small candle to maintain the chocolate at just the right temperature.

8 ounces (225 g) semi-sweet
   chocolate (70% cocoa solids,
   if possible), broken into pieces
finely grated zest of ½ orange
¾ cup (185 ml) heavy cream
1 tablespoon (15 g) unsalted butter
2 tablespoons Cointreau or other
   orange-flavoured liqueur

For dipping:
fresh, chilled firm fruits, such as
   strawberries, figs, apricot halves,
   peach slices, bananas, kiwi fruit,
   and cherries

1 Put the chocolate into the La Saucière fondue pot and melt over a low heat on the stovetop. Add the orange zest, cream, and butter as the chocolate begins to melt. Keep stirring until all the ingredients are melted. Stir in the Cointreau.

2 Transfer the fondue pot to its stand above the lit candle flame to keep it warm. Stir occasionally if not serving immediately.

Any of the larger fondue sets can be used for this recipe but do remember to keep the burner flame very low to avoid burning the chocolate.

Allow approximately 2 ounces (60 g) of dipping ingredients per person.

CHERRY AND KIRSCH FONDUE

Serves 6
Preparation time: 5 minutes
Cooking time: 10 minutes

This makes a delightful dessert to serve on cold winter days.

1 pound (450 g) canned red
    cherries, pitted
1 pound (450 g) canned black
    cherries, pitted
2 tablespoons white sugar
4 tablespoons kirsch
1 tablespoon cornstarch
½ cup (125 ml) plain fromage frais
    or heavy cream

For dipping:
small shortbread or macaroon
    cookies
marshmallows
baby meringues

1 Drain the juice from both cans of cherries into the fondue pot. Cut the cherries into halves and add to the juices. Stir in the sugar and kirsch, stirring to dissolve the sugar.

2 Place the fondue pot over medium heat on the stovetop to warm the mixture through.

3 Blend the cornstarch with a little water, then stir into the cherries and cook, stirring, until thickened. Turn off the heat and stir in the fromage frais or heavy cream.

4 Transfer the pot to the fondue stand with the lit spirit burner and stir occasionally.

FONDUE BOURGUIGNONNE

Serves 6

**Preparation time: 10 minutes
+ making the sauces (optional)**

Cooking time: while eating

*This is the traditional meat fondue
that features good-quality steak.
However, mixed meat fondues are
also popular and can be made
using this method (see Cook's
Tips, below).*

*The meat can be prepared
several hours in advance and then
be served very simply with baked
potatoes and salads. Offer a
selection of at least three dipping
sauces, all of which can be bought
if you don't want to take the time to
make any.*

2¼ pounds (1 kg) good-quality
    steak, such as filet and sirloin,
    1-inch (2.5 cm) thick
about 2⅓ cups (580 ml) peanut or
    vegetable oil, for frying
1 bay leaf, torn in half
1 garlic clove, cut in half
dipping sauces, such as Béarnaise
    sauce, mustard, and tomato
    relish, to serve

1 Prepare the meat by
trimming away any fat or gristle and
cutting into 1-inch (2.5 cm) cubes.
Dry well with paper towel before
plating or frying.

2 Heat the oil in the fondue pot
over a medium heat on the
stovetop until it reaches 375°F
(190°C). Use a thermometer to
check the temperature, or test by
dropping a small cube of dry bread
into the hot oil; it should turn
golden brown in less than a
minute. If the oil smokes, remove
the pot from the heat and set aside
while the oil cools.

3 Carefully transfer the hot
fondue pot with the oil to the stand
with the lit spirit burner and adjust
the flame to maintain the correct
frying temperature.

4 Drop in the bay leaf and
garlic halves for extra flavoring.

5 Each person cooks their
own selection of meat. The meat is
extremely hot when first removed
from the oil, therefore it should be
removed from the fork and left to
cool slightly before being eaten
with the dipping sauces.

*Do not attempt to overfill the
fondue pot with the oil. The
maximum filling level must be no
more than one-third full.*

*Do not leave heating or hot
oil unattended at any time.*

*Make sure the meat is dry
before cooking, as any moisture*

*going into the hot oil causes excessive
spitting and will cool the oil too quickly.*

*Small sausages, slab-bacon cubes,
chicken livers, diced lean pork, chicken,
or turkey can also be used. It can be
nice to offer each person a selection of
meat on their own plate.*

*A spicy, full-bodied red made
from Zinfandel or Syrah will make
an excellent match for the steak.
If pork or chicken are used, look
for a medium-bodied red such as
Pinot Noir.*

PÂTÉ TERRINES

When is a pâté a pâté, or when is it a terrine? Actually, in modern terms, they are the same thing. "Terrine" simply denotes the name of the dish, the "shape" they are cooked in. In France you may be served a pâté where the meats and vegetables are encased in a pastry crust, as this is, historically, the correct definition for this type of recipe; outside France this would usually be called a pie. "Pâté en terrine", however, describes the recipe we have now come to expect, with meats or vegetables (either finely or coarsely mixed) cooked or set into a shape for slicing cold.

Whether a recipe is called a "pâté" or a "terrine" now appears to be down to the author of the recipe but, in very general terms, pâtés tend to have finer minced textures, whereas terrines are often coarser or have whole pieces of food in them, such as the asparagus in the Salmon and Asparagus Terrine on page 115. Pâtés and terrines have become very popular over recent years in delicatessens as well as restaurants, where they are often "signature" dishes. Unlike the original recipes, which are almost always made from fairly rich meats, fat, wine and herbs, more modern recipes often include vegetables, cheese or fish.

For the less experienced cook, the prospect of making a pâté or terrine may seem off-putting, not least because of the time needed to prepare the ingredients. But, fortunately, today we have food processors and blenders, so even the most arduous chopping tasks can be reduced to a few seconds. Once the preparation is done, it's simply a case of assembling the ingredients by mixing or layering and, if the layers in the final result are not quite as perfect as they could be, it doesn't really matter because the flavor of your home-made recipe will be so enjoyable.

However, the real key to success is of course the dish itself, and the Le Creuset pâté terrine dish has been specially designed for the job. Pâtés and terrines often require gentle temperatures to ensure even cooking. Cast iron is ideal, because it allows a gentle but even spread of heat throughout the whole dish. The shape itself is all-important, and the Le Creuset dish allows for good even-sized slices to be made. The dish has a well-fitting lid which sits "snugly" on the rim so that moisture is retained. However, because some recipes contain ingredients with a lot more fat or water, the small hole in the lid vents out a tiny amount of steam when necessary, thereby keeping the contents balanced and not too wet or steamy. Not all pâtés or terrines have to be turned out and instead can be served straight from the dish. If this is the case and there is pâté left for another day, it can be stored and chilled quite safely in the dish with its porcelain enamel surface. Even the strongest garlic flavors or wines in the mixture will do it no harm. Not all pâtés or terrines have to be cooked and there are more and more recipes where the ingredients are set in their own juices or set with a little gelatin. These may be delicate, sweet flavors and to make one of these immediately after making a garlic-flavored pâté is no trouble at all; there will be no flavor transfer.

But, as with most pieces of Le Creuset, the pâté terrine dish has its "other side" and perhaps this "other side" is completely overlooked, which is a great pity because it is so useful.

The shape is ideal for making cakes such as fruit loaves, seed cake or gingerbread. The material allows the even rising and baking which a good cake mold should give and the final result can be neatly sliced. The recipe for Moist Lemon and Coconut Cake on page 120 has filled many lunch boxes leaving my home.

Bread also bakes very well in this shape; a good family-size loaf is produced. The simple "one step" mixing and rising technique I use requires no previous bread-making skills, just the urge to produce those tantalizing bread-baking aromas. And last, but not least, the pâté terrine dish is perfect for meat loaf whether you serve it hot or cold. The dish holds approximately 2¼ pounds (1 kg) of meat mixture, so any of your own recipes can be adapted to fit. The recipes in this chapter are quite varied but will give you a glimpse of the many ways a pâté terrine dish can be used.

General Tips

- Many cooked meat or fish pâtés require the dish to be placed in a "bain-marie". This simply means placing the covered pâté terrine dish inside a much larger one containing water. The water level should generally reach about half-way up the side walls of the pâté terrine dish and be topped up with hot water if necessary. A bain-marie is often used for pâtés and terrines as it allows the mixture to cook very gently without coloring and baking, resulting in a texture that is the same all the way through.
- When making cooked pâtés or terrines, the dish can be greased but there is no need to line it with parchment paper. Sometimes the dish is lined with bacon and this acts as a casing for the pâté.
- Uncooked "set" pâtés or terrines do not need the dish to be lined, unless it is required to be turned out "whole", when lining with strips of parchment paper or plastic wrap will aid the ease of release.
- Generally, when baking cakes and bread the dish simply requires greasing and flouring. However, if used for very soft or light cake mixtures, lining with a strip of parchment paper will make turning out easier. The lid is not used when baking cakes or bread.
- Always allow the dish to cool for at least 10 to15 minutes before turning hot foods out, and use a cloth or oven mitts for lifting, as it will still be hot.
- If any ingredients need to be melted or cooked in the dish, this can be done over a medium or low heat setting on the stovetop.

COARSE COUNTRY PÂTÉ

Makes 12 to 14 slices
Preparation time: 30 minutes
Cooking time: 2 to 2½ hours

This pâté has bold peppery flavors and a firm, coarse texture. The outer wrapping of the bacon and bay leaves is not difficult to do and makes the finished dish so attractive for a lunch or buffet table. This recipe uses the 1½-quart (32 cm) pâté terrine dish.

8 ounces (225 g) bacon
4 bay leaves
12 ounces (350 g) ground lean
   pork
8 ounces (225 g) boneless
   chicken thigh meat, chopped
   finely
8 ounces (225 g) chicken livers,
   chopped
2 shallots, chopped finely
2 garlic cloves, crushed
1 tablespoon mixed whole
   peppercorns
1 tablespoon fresh chopped thyme
1 tablespoon fresh chopped sage
1 teaspoon salt
¼ teaspoon freshly ground black
   pepper
3 large eggs
3 tablespoons brandy

1 Thin the bacon by pressing it out on a board with a round-bladed knife. Lay the four bay leaves along the bottom of the dish, then line the bottom and sides with the bacon positioned side by side. Leave a little of the bacon overhanging the sides of the dish; reserve any extra bacon.

2 Preheat the oven to 300°F/150°C/Gas Mark 2. Put the pork, chicken, and chicken livers into a bowl with all the other ingredients. Stir together thoroughly. Transfer the mixture to the lined dish, leveling the top. Use the overhanging pieces of bacon and any reserved bacon to enclose the pâté.

3 Put on the lid and stand the pâté terrine dish in a bain-marie (see General Tips on page 113).

4 Bake the pâté in the oven for 2 to 2½ hours, or until the juices in the middle of the pâté run clear when pierced with a turkey skewer or toothpick. Remove the pâté terrine dish from the bain-marie and set aside to cool completely before unmolding. Leave the lid on as the pâté cools. Unmold onto a large serving dish, trimming away any meat solids that have escaped. Cut into even slices with a very sharp knife.

 This recipe can also be cooked in a 2-quart (18 cm) French oven.

 Turkey meat can be used instead of chicken.
This recipe freezes well for up to 1 month. Thaw completely before use.

 A red Burgundy or Oregon Pinot Noir will make a good partner for the pâté and can stand up to its assertive flavor.

SALMON AND ASPARAGUS TERRINE WITH HERB MAYONNAISE

Makes 12 to 14 slices

Preparation time: 30 minutes + 6 hours chilling

Cooking time: 10 minutes for poaching the fresh salmon

This is a very pretty terrine to serve. This recipe uses the 1½-quart (32 cm) pâté terrine dish.

10 ounces (300 g) young, fresh asparagus tips

12 ounces (350 g) smoked salmon, sliced thinly

5 teaspoons unflavored powdered gelatin

1 pound 10 ounces (750 g) salmon fillet, cooked

1 tablespoon fresh chopped dill

1 tablespoon fresh chopped cilantro

½ teaspoon cayenne pepper

finely grated zest of 1 lemon

4 tablespoons lemon juice

1 cup (250 ml) heavy cream

salt and freshly ground black pepper

a few small, fresh dressed salad leaves, to garnish

For the herb mayonnaise:

6 tablespoons mayonnaise

1 tablespoon chopped fresh dill

1 tablespoon chopped fresh cilantro

1 teaspoon lemon juice

1 Line the pâté terrine dish with a large sheet of plastic wrap that generously overlaps the top edges. Smooth the bottom the best you can because this will be the top when you unmold the terrine.

2 Trim any woody ends from the asparagus. Boil or steam until just tender, then drain well and rinse in cold water.

3 Use the slices of smoked salmon to completely line the pâté terrine dish, leaving a little to hang over the top rim; reserve the odd-shaped pieces to cover the mixture, once the dish is filled.

4 Sprinkle the gelatin into a small bowl containing 3 tablespoons of very hot water and stir until it is completely dissolved. Set aside to cool slightly.

5 Put the salmon into a food processor or blender with the herbs, cayenne, lemon zest and juice and process for 10 seconds until blended, but not absolutely smooth. Add the cream, and dissolved gelatin, and season to taste. Blend again for 5 seconds only.

6 Spoon half the salmon mixture into the pâté terrine dish, levelling the surface. Arrange the asparagus in a single layer, alternating the spears tips and stems and packing the pieces closely together.

7 Cover with the remaining salmon and level again. Use the overlapping pieces of smoked salmon to enclose the mixture and fill any gaps with the reserved pieces.

8 Cover the top with the overlapping plastic wrap and chill for at least 6 hours.

9 While the terrine is setting, prepare the mayonnaise. Put all the ingredients into a bowl and mix thoroughly. Cover and chill until required.

10 Unmold the terrine onto a large serving plate and remove the plastic wrap. Cut into even slices using a very sharp knife, wiping the blade between slices. Garnish each portion with a few small, fresh, dressed salad leaves and a spoonful of the mayonnaise.

Slices of smoked trout can be used instead of the smoked salmon.

Low-fat whipping cream can be used instead of the heavy cream.

This terrine does not freeze well, because it becomes watery when it thaws.

ONE-STEP ONION AND OLIVE BREAD

Makes 12 slices

Preparation time: 20 minutes + rising time

Cooking time: 35 to 40 minutes

The smell of freshly-baked homemade bread is hard to beat, but the thought of making it can be daunting. However there is no need to feel that way because with a single mixing and rising recipe such as this, no previous bread-making experience is necessary. This recipe uses the 1½-quart (32 cm) pâté terrine as a bread mold.

1 medium onion, chopped finely
3 tablespoons olive oil
6 cups (750 g) white bread flour
1 teaspoon salt
½ teaspoon freshly ground black
    pepper
1 envelope of active-dry yeast
½ cup (125 ml) milk
½ cup (60 g) pitted ripe olives,
    chopped roughly
1 teaspoon coarse sea salt

1 Grease and flour the inside of the pâté terrine dish; the lid is not used for this recipe.

2 Put the onion and 1 tablespoon of the oil into a microwave bowl, cover, and microwave on full power for 1½ to 2 minutes, until the onion is soft. Set aside to cool.

3 Sift the flour and salt into a large bowl and stir in the pepper and yeast.

4 Put 1½ cups (375 ml) very hot water in a bowl and add the cold milk to give the correct temperature for mixing. Add the remaining oil as well.

5 Stir the onions and olives into the dry ingredients, then gradually stir in the liquid. The dough should be slightly wet, but not sticky; if it seems too dry add a little more milk. Turn out the dough on to a well-floured surface and knead for 1 to 2 minutes. Form it into a long roll about the length of the pâté terrine dish.

6 Transfer the dough to the dish with any seams or folds tucked underneath. Make a few slashes across the top of the dough. Brush the top with a little olive oil. Cover loosely with plastic wrap and leave for 1 to 1½ hours in a warm place to rise until the dough is just above the rim. Sprinkle with the salt just before baking. Preheat the oven to 375°F/190°C/Gas Mark 5.

7 Bake the bread in the middle of the oven for 35 to 40 minutes until risen and golden brown. Leave to cool in the dish for 10 minutes before unmolding on a cooling rack.

Replace the olives with ½ cup (50 g) sun-dried tomatoes for a change of flavor.

If you like a really soft crust, cover the freshly baked, warm bread with a clean dish towel while it cools.

PORK AND VEGETABLE LOAF

Makes 10 to 12 slices
Preparation time: 20 minutes
Cooking time: 1 hour

A well-flavored meatloaf can be such a good recipe to make for picnics, parties, or snack lunches. The seasoning is important and should be quite strong at the beginning because it lessens once baked. To check the seasoning, fry a small patty shape of the meat in a skillet and taste. You can then also decide if the texture is too crumbly and you need to add an extra egg. This recipe uses the 1½-quart (32 cm) pâté terrine dish.

2¼ pounds (1 kg) lean ground pork
1 large onion, chopped finely
2 cups (125 g) dried white bread crumbs
1 cup (125 g) finely chopped bacon
1 small red bell pepper, seeded and chopped
1 cup (125 g) thin green beans, trimmed and cut into ¼-inch (5 mm) pieces
2 teaspoons dried parsley
2 teaspoons dried thyme
4 or 5 large eggs, beaten
1¼ teaspoons salt

½ teaspoon freshly ground black pepper

To serve:

potatoes or salad

1   Grease the inside of the pâté terrine dish well and place a strip of parchment paper along the bottom and up the short sides; this helps to release the meatloaf when it is hot.

2   Preheat the oven to 350°F/180°C/Gas Mark 4. Put all the ingredients, including only 4 eggs, into a large bowl and mix thoroughly. Fry a small amount of the mixture in a skillet and taste to check the seasoning and consistency. Adjust the seasoning, if necessary, and beat in an extra egg if the mixture is too crumbly.

3   Pack the meatloaf mixture firmly into the pâté terrine dish, levelling the top.

4   Cover with the lightly greased lid and bake in the middle of the oven for 40 to 45 minutes. Remove the lid and continue baking for 15 minutes longer, or until the top is brown. Use a turkey skewer or toothpick to check the middle is cooked. The juices should run clear.

5   Leave the meatloaf to cool in the dish for 10 minutes, then drain off the excess fat or juices. Unmold onto a board, peel off the lining paper, and leave to rest, covered with aluminum foil for 10 minutes before slicing thickly. This meatloaf is good hot or cold, served with potatoes or salad.

To reduce the fat content of this recipe, gently fry the pork for 4 to 5 minutes in a skillet before mixing with the other ingredients.

To serve cold, leave the meatloaf to cool completely in the pâté terrine dish, then ease around the sides with a round-blade knife before turning out.

VEGETABLE AND CHEESE TERRINE

Makes 10 to 12 slices

Preparation time: 30 minutes + overnight chilling

Cooking time: 50 to 55 minutes

This light and very attractive terrine uses young fresh vegetables, cheese, and eggs to make an excellent main course dish or buffet centerpiece. It is best made a day in advance because it is easiest to slice when chilled. This recipe uses the 1½-quart (32 cm) pâté terrine dish.

8 ounces (225 g) young carrots
2 celery stalks
6 ounces (175 g) thin green beans
1½ cups (225 g) shelled, young peas
5 large eggs
¼ teaspoon salt
⅛ teaspoon freshly ground black pepper
¼ teaspoon ground nutmeg
1½ cups (175 g) coarsely grated Gruyère cheese
1 cup (250 ml) heavy cream
1 tablespoon chopped fresh flat-leaf parsley
a little butter, for greasing

1 Prepare all the vegetables. Cut the carrots and celery into fine julienne strips approximately 1½ inches (3 cm) long. Trim the beans and cut these into pieces the same length: keep all the vegetables separate as they are prepared.

2 Blanch each type of vegetable separately, one after the other, in lightly salted, boiling water for 3 minutes each. Immediately drain them and plunge into ice-cold water to retain their color and texture. Dry off any excess moisture with paper towels.

3 In a large bowl, beat the eggs thoroughly with the seasonings and nutmeg. Add the cheese, cream, and parsley, mixing well.

4 Preheat the oven to 325°F/160°C/Gas Mark 3. Lightly grease the inside of the pâté terrine dish. Put a layer of peas in the bottom, spreading them evenly. Add about one-quarter of the egg mixture, followed by a layer of carrots. Add another quarter of egg mixture, then the green beans and another quarter of the egg mixture. Add the celery and then the remaining egg mixture.

5 Cover the dish with the lid and place in a bain-marie, allowing the water to come half-way up the sides of the dish. Place in the oven and cook for 40 minutes. Remove the lid and continue cooking for 10 to 15 minutes longer until the terrine is just set in the middle and slightly springy to the touch.

6 Remove the dish from the bain-marie and leave to cool completely. Cover and chill overnight. To unmold, ease a metal spatula around the edges, then invert on to a large serving plate. Slice with a really sharp knife, wiping the blade between slices.

Low-fat whipping cream can be used for this recipe. Cheeses other than Gruyère also work well in this recipe. Try Cheddar or Monterey Jack, for example.

This recipe does not freeze well because the texture becomes watery when thawed.

MOIST LEMON AND COCONUT CAKE

Makes 12 to 14 slices

Preparation time: 20 minutes + cooling

Cooking time: 45 minutes

This moist cake is extremely simple to make using the "one-step" method in a food processor. This recipe uses the 1½-quart (32 cm) pâté terrine dish as a cake mold.

For the cake:

2 sticks (225 g) butter or
   margarine, softened
1 cup (225 g) superfine granulated
   sugar
3 large eggs
2 cups (250 g) sifted self-rising
   flour
1 teaspoon baking powder
finely grated zest of 2 lemons
3 tablespoons lemon juice
½ cup (40 g) shredded coconut,
   not packed

For the glaze:

6 tablespoons confectioners' sugar
3 tablespoons lemon juice

1 Preheat the oven to 325°F/160°C/Gas Mark 3. Grease and flour the interior of the pâté terrine dish; the lid is not used for this recipe.

2 Put the butter or margarine, sugar, eggs, flour, and baking powder into a food processor and process for approximately 10 seconds. Scrape down the sides, add the lemon zest, lemon juice and coconut. Process again for 10 seconds but do not overmix.

3 Spoon the batter into the prepared dish and level the top, making a shallow groove along the length of the mixture in the middle.

4 Bake in the middle of the oven for 30 minutes, then reduce the temperature to 300°F/150°C/Gas Mark 2 and continue baking for 15 minutes longer until the cake is risen and golden brown. Test if the cake is cooked through by piercing the middle with a turkey skewer or toothpick. It will come out cleanly when the mixture is cooked.

5 Leave the cake to cool in the dish for 10 minutes before turning it out. Cool on a cake rack.

6 To make the glaze, put the confectioners' sugar into a bowl and gradually blend in the lemon juice, beating until smooth. When the cake is cool, brush the glaze all over the top and sides of the cake.

 If you don't have a processor, place all the ingredients for the cake in a large bowl and beat until smooth.
   For the best results, bake this cake a day in advance and *store overnight in an airtight container before slicing.*

STRAWBERRY-CHEESE REFRIGERATOR CAKE

Makes 12 to 14 slices

Preparation time: 25 minutes + overnight setting and chilling

Cooking time: none

This dessert is rich, but there are occasions when indulgence is perhaps allowed! It requires ample time to set and chill, so it is best made a day ahead. This recipe uses the 1½-quart (32 cm) pâté terrine dish as a cake mold.

3½ cups (350 g) Graham cracker crumbs, packed

1½ sticks (175 g) unsalted butter, melted

5 teaspoons unflavored powdered gelatin

12 ounces (350 g) fresh strawberries, hulled

12 ounces (350 g) cream cheese

½ cup (125 ml) heavy cream

about 1 tablespoon white sugar

mint leaves (optional), to garnish

1 Line the pâté terrine dish with a large piece of plastic wrap that generously overlaps the top edges of the dish. Smooth the bottom as best as you can because this will be the top when you unmold the cake.

2 Mix the crumbs with the butter and set aside to cool completely.

3 Sprinkle the gelatin into a small bowl containing 3 tablespoons of very hot water and stir until it is completely dissolved. Set aside to cool slightly.

4 Reserve 6 of the best strawberries for decoration and purée the remainder.

5 Beat together the cheese, cream, strawberry purée, and 1 tablespoon of sugar, adding a little extra sugar if you prefer more sweetness. Stir in the dissolved gelatin.

6 Put half of the strawberry-cheese batter in the bottom of the dish, leveling the surface. Add half

the crumbs, spreading them over the mixture evenly and lightly. Add the remaining strawberry batter, again leveling the surface, and then the second layer of crumbs. Bring the edges of the plastic wrap up and over to cover the top.

7 Place in the refrigerator and chill for at least 6 hours, but preferably overnight.

8 Unmold the cake onto a large serving plate and remove the plastic wrap. Decorate the top with the reserved strawberries, cut in half, and add some fresh mint leaves if available. Keep chilled until ready to serve; it slices best when really cold.

Raspberries or blueberries can be used for this recipe instead of the strawberries.

Slice with a really sharp knife, wiping the blade between slices.

This recipe does not freeze well, because the strawberry-cheese layers can seep juice when it is thawed.

SAUCEPANS

In France where the heritage of the "saucepan" began, their use, as one would expect, is still mainly confined to making sauces. French cooks are renowned for their sauce-making skills and appreciate the difference a good sauce can make to a quite simple dish. Even today, saucepans in France are usually sold without lids because most sauces need stirring and attention, not covering and leaving.

As far as sauce-making is concerned, a Le Creuset cast iron saucepan has everything you need: a sturdy design, not too deep, a good thick base, a smooth and curved inner surface that makes stirring and cleaning simplicity itself and a shaped pouring lip. However, outside France, sauce-making is not the only role we expect a saucepan to play and it has become an almost vital piece of our everyday cooking equipment. We turn to it for cooking pasta, boiling vegetables, making frostings and caramel and so much more. With so many uses, a good saucepan also has to be well balanced and stable on any heat source and perform well at very low and gentle temperatures as well as being efficient for quick boiling.

Le Creuset saucepans offer a choice of handle styles: integrated metal, which is the most traditional and allows the pan to go into the oven to double as a casserole dish, or heat-resistant black phenolic plastic. This handle is softly contoured in shape and can be washed, like the iron-handle version, in the dishwasher.

Saucepans range in size from the 1-quart (16 cm) iron-handle saucepan to the 2-quart (20 cm) iron-handle or phenolic-handle pan. The iron-handle "Windsor" saucepan is a speciality shape with a deeper side wall. With its well-fitting lid, it is suited for simmering sauces and then open-boiling to concentrate flavors and consistency.

As with all other Le Creuset pieces, saucepans are best used on medium and low heats and this is particularly important if a delicate sauce is being made. But they can be used on high heats when boiling water for vegetables or pasta.

The recipes in this chapter cover just a few of the best-loved sauces and those that follow the French example – a good well-flavored sauce that transforms the simplest of ingredients into something special.

General Tips

- Do not overfill a saucepan. A general rule is no more than two-thirds full so that the boiling or simmering level can be maintained without the contents boiling over.
- Use plastic, wooden, or Le Creuset heat-resistant silicone spoons and spatulas for stirring. These are infinitely more comfortable and will not scratch or damage the porcelain enamel surface. However, occasional careful use of a metal spoon is acceptable.
- Do not, however, use electric hand held mixer blades in a saucepan or bang metal spoons or blades on the top rim of the pan. Repeated abuse in this way will eventually damage the porcelain enamel causing tiny flaws that may give way to rust.
- If you do have an accident and boil a pan dry – and it happens to us all – don't be too alarmed. Simply remove the pan from the heat and leave it to cool until it is comfortable to touch. Fill it with warm water and a little washing up liquid or machine clothes washing powder and return it to the heat to boil. It may take several "boilings" to ease the burnt food from the base but it usually works. At no time try prodding or scrapping the blackened area with a blade or metal cleaning pad. Once clean, the surface can be re-conditioned and given a final polish with the special Le Creuset cookware cleaner.

HOLLANDAISE SAUCE

Serves 6

Preparation time: 10 minutes

Cooking time: 15 to 20 minutes

A simple broiled fish steak, whether it be cod, flounder, or salmon, is transformed into a very special dish when served with a little freshly-made hollandaise. This sauce is also good served with fresh vegetables, such as steamed asparagus or globe artichokes. This sauce should not be kept hot for longer than 15 to 20 minutes before serving, otherwise the consistency can separate and become oily. This recipe uses the 2-quart (20 cm) saucepan.

4 tablespoons lemon juice
4 large egg yolks
2 sticks (225 g) unsalted butter, softened
a little salt and freshly ground black pepper

1 Put a heatproof bowl over the saucepan so that it rests on the rim. Put sufficient water in the saucepan so it is just under, but not touching, the bottom of the bowl. Bring this water to a simmer and maintain at a simmer, not a rapid boil.

2 Put the lemon juice, 2 teaspoons of water, and seasoning into the bowl. Beat in the egg yolks and a small piece of the butter, beating lightly until the consistency thickens.

3 Add the remaining butter, a little at a time, beating the sauce well between additions.

4 When all the butter has been incorporated the sauce should be thick and glossy. Taste and adjust the seasoning before serving. To keep the sauce warm for no more than 15 to 20 minutes, remove the pan with the bowl from the heat and cover the sauce with a piece of wet, crumpled baking parchment paper.

If the sauce begins to curdle, it is probably due to the heat being too high, or the butter being added too quickly. Remove from the heat and beat well before proceeding.

If the sauce does separate on standing, beat in a tablespoon of cold water before serving.

CLASSIC TOMATO AND BASIL SAUCE

Serves 6
Preparation time: 10 minutes
Cooking time: 45 minutes

This is just a very good basic sauce to use with pasta on its own, or mixed with other ingredients. It also makes a good tomato topping for homemade pizza or Italian bruschettas. This recipe uses the 2-quart (20 cm) saucepan.

3 tablespoons extra-virgin olive oil
1 medium onion, chopped finely
2 celery stalks, chopped finely
1 carrot, grated coarsely
2 large garlic cloves, crushed
2 pounds (900 g) canned plum
  tomatoes, chopped with their
  juice
a large handful of fresh basil leaves
salt and freshly ground black
  pepper
a pat of butter, to finish

1 Heat the oil in the saucepan over a medium heat on the stovetop. Add the onion, celery, and carrot and cook very gently for 4 to 5 minutes without letting the ingredients color. Add the garlic and fry for 1 minute longer.

2 Add the tomatoes, roughly torn basil leaves, and plenty of seasoning. Cover and simmer, stirring occasionally, for 30 to 40 minutes until the vegetables are tender.

3 Uncover the pan, increase the heat, and boil gently for 5 to 10 minutes to thicken.

4 Use the sauce as it is in this "chunky" consistency, or purée in a food processor. Whichever texture you choose, stir the butter into the sauce just before serving; it rounds off the flavors and makes the sauce smoother.

 This sauce can also be made in the round 2¾-quart (20 cm) French oven.

 This sauce freezes well. Chill thoroughly, then freeze in useful quantities.

Fresh, softer tomatoes can be used instead of canned ones. Remove their skins by plunging into boiling water for 1 minute, then into cold for 1 minute. Add 2 teaspoons of tomato paste to the saucepan in Step 2 to make a stronger colored sauce.

Add 2 or 3 tablespoons of dry white wine for extra richness.

CRÈME ANGLAISE

Serves 4 to 6
Preparation time: 5 minutes
Cooking time: 15 minutes

A heavy-bottomed saucepan is a must for this type of custard sauce, which needs to be cooked gently and slowly. Rushing it will spoil the texture. As a safeguard, this recipe includes a little cornstarch, which prevents the mixture from curdling if the eggs get too hot. Although this recipe requires a little care, it is worth the effort. This recipe uses the 2-quart (20 cm) saucepan.

1½ cups (375 ml) milk
2 teaspoons vanilla extract
4 large egg yolks
¼ cup (60 g) white sugar
1 teaspoon cornstarch

1 Put the milk and vanilla extract into the saucepan. Place over a medium heat on the stovetop and heat until the milk is just below the simmering point.

2 Beat together the egg yolks, sugar, and cornstarch. Pour the hot milk onto the egg mixture, stirring all the time.

3 Rinse out the pan with warm water and return the sauce mixture to it. Place over low heat and cook, stirring constantly, until the sauce is smooth and thick. Serve immediately with pies and other desserts, or serve chilled (see Cook's Tips, below).

CHOCOLATE SAUCE

Serves 6 to 8
Preparation time: 5 minutes
Cooking time: 10 minutes

This is an indispensable chocolate sauce, which once made can be stored in the refrigerator for up to two weeks. Use over ice cream or profiteroles, or as a filling for cakes. It is very rich, but has a slight bitterness from the coffee that is added. This recipe uses the 1½-quart (18 cm) saucepan.

6 ounces (175 g) semi-sweet chocolate, broken into pieces
2 tablespoons light corn syrup
1 teaspoon instant coffee powder or granules
1 tablespoon (15 g) butter, softened
3 tablespoons crème fraîche or sour cream

1 Put the chocolate in the saucepan over a low heat with the syrup, coffee, and butter, stirring all the time until all the ingredients melt and are thoroughly mixed.

2 Remove the saucepan from the heat and leave the sauce to cool for 5 to 10 minutes. Beat in the crème fraîche or sour cream, then pour into a serving bowl or dish. It can be served warm, or left to cool completely when it will thicken and can then be used like whipped cream.

 To use chilled, transfer the sauce to a bowl and cover the top with a piece of wet, crumpled parchment baking paper, which will prevent a skin forming. Transfer to the refrigerator and chill for up to 2 or 3 hours. Use within 48 hours of making.
   Crème Anglaise can also be made thicker to use chilled as a filling for cakes and tarts. Add 2 tablespoons cornstarch instead of 1 teaspoon. Cool and chill as above.

 If storing in the refrigerator, place in a bowl and cool before covering with plastic wrap. As the sauce is required, microwave the amount you need on full power for 10 to 20 seconds to soften and warm through.
   To use as a cake frosting or filling, use straight from the refrigerator when it will be firm and set. It is very rich, so spread it thinly.

Round French Oven

L2501-18	2 qt
L2501-20	2¾ qt
L2501-22	3½ qt
L2501-24	4½ qt
L2501-26	5½ qt
L2501-28	7 qt
L2501-30	8¾ qt
L2501-34	13 qt

Oval French Oven

L2502-25	3½ qt
L2502-29	5 qt
L2502-31	6½ qt
L2502-35	9½ qt

Windsor Saucepan

L2526-00	1½ qt

Iron Handle Saucepan

L2507-16	1 qt
L2507-20	2 qt

Phenolic Handle Saucepan

L2939-18	1½ qt
L2939-20	2 qt

Multi-Function Pan

L2531-18	1 qt
L2531-22	2 qt
L2531-26	3 qt

Nonstick Omelette Pan

L2036-20C	⅞ qt

Phenolic Handle Nonstick Frypan

L2858-24	1 qt
L2858-28	2¾ qt

Phenolic Handle Nonstick Sauté Pan

L2859-24	2¼ qt
L2859-28	3¾ qt

Domed Glass Lid

L3759-24	9½"
L3759-28	11"

Iron Handle Skillet

L2024-23	1¼ qt
L2024-26	1⅞ qt
L2024-30	2½ qt

Breakfast/Brunch Griddle

L2095	10"

Oblong Skillet Grill

L2022-32	2⅜ qt

Round Skillet Grill

L2023-26	1⅞ qt
L2023-30	2½ qt

Square Skillet Grill

L2021-26	2¼ qt

Mini Wok

L25W1-28	2¼ qt

Wok	L25W1-36	4¼ qt

Pumpkin Casserole	L2538-02	2 qt

Heart Casserole	L25C1-02	2 qt

Moroccan Tagine	L7473-00	1½ qt

Buffet Casserole	L2532-26	2½ qt
	L2532-30	3½ qt

Soup Pot	L2574-22	2⅝ qt

Bouillabaisse Pot	L2574-32	7¼ qt

Oval Au Gratin	L0013-28	1½ qt
	L0013-36	2⅝ qt

Roaster	L2011-30	2½ qt
	L2011-40	6½ qt

Pâté Terrine	L0524-32	1½ qt

Tatin Dish Anniversary Pan	L2129-25	1½ qt

Square Baker	L2540-18	2 qt

La Saucière	L6800	¾ qt

Traditional Fondue	LA080	1½ qt

Compact Fondue	L6011	2¼ qt

Lifetime Warranty

Le Creuset is proud of the workmanship in its products and warrantees its enameled Cast Iron Cookware, from the date of purchase, for the lifetime of the original owner, whether a self-purchase or received as a gift.

The Lifetime Warranty covers faulty workmanship and materials when the product is used in normal domestic household conditions and in accordance with the care and use instructions provided.

Stovetops

All Le Creuset enameled Cast Iron, or enamel on steel stock pots and tea kettles can be used with confidence on any stovetop – gas, electric, induction and ceramic.

Colors and Shapes

Le Creuset is renowned for its wide range of color finishes and shapes and many are featured in this book. To see a full range of both, visit a Le Creuset Company store.

Full details of the Lifetime Warranty are supplied in the booklet that accompanies each piece at the time of purchase. A further copy and other information can be obtained from CONSUMER SERVICES. Call toll free 1-877-CREUSET (2738738) or write to Le Creuset of America Inc., PO Box 67, 114 Bob Gifford Boulevard, Early Branch, South Carolina 29916.